The Brave Ones

The Journals and Letters of the 1911-1912 Expedition Down the Green and Colorado Rivers by

Ellsworth L. Kolb and Emery C. Kolb

including the journal of Hubert R. Lauzon

other books by William C. Suran

THE KOLB BROTHERS OF GRAND CANYON
Being a Collection of Tales of High Adventure,
Memorable Incidents, & Humerous Anecdotes
Grand Canyon Natural History Association

WITH THE WINGS OF AN ANGEL
A Biography of Ellsworth and Emery Kolb
Photographers of Grand Canyon
on-line at Grand Canyon Historical Society

related books by Fretwater Press

THE DOING OF THE THING
The Brief, Brilliant Whitewater
Career of Buzz Holmstrom
by Vince Welch, Cort Conley, and Brad Dimock

SUNK WITHOUT A SOUND
The Tragic Colorado River Honeymoon
of Glen and Bessie Hyde
by Brad Dimock

Colorado River Chronicles Series

I   THE BRAVE ONES

II   EVERY RAPID SPEAKS PLAINLY
The Salmon, Green, and Colorado
River Journals of Buzz Holmstrom
Brad Dimock, editor

ONCE A JOURNEY is designed, equipped and put in process, a new factor takes over. A trip, a safari, an expedition, is an entity different from all other journeys. It has personality, temperament, individuality, uniqueness. A journey is a person in itself, no two are alike. And all plans, safeguards, policing and coercion are fruitless. We find after years of struggle that we do not take a trip; a trip takes us. Tour masters, schedules, reservations, brass-bound and inevitable, dash themselves into wreckage on the personality of the trip. In this a journey is like a marriage; the certain way to be wrong is to think you control it.

— JOHN STEINBECK

The Brave Ones

Plunging down the Colorado
In dark canyons every day
It was pleasant an old timer
To meet along the way.

Dropping gold pan there he hailed us
"Come ashore boys, what's the news?
Is but two all of your party,
Or what number did you lose?"

So we anchored, as t'was evening
And the information gave
Then he slapped us on the shoulder
And said, "Boys, you're mighty brave."

"I've had comrades," he continued,
"That in yonder waves were tossed
And I'm working now alone boys,
Needn't tell you they were lost."

"Yes, 'tis wicked," I admitted
"But should this water be our grave,
There are others of our party,
And 'tis they you should call brave."

Now imagine if you're able
This grim old timer's look
As I handed him a picture
I had kept in my note book.

"Ah, the brave ones!" said the miner,
"I understand the tale
'Tis an anxious wife and baby
Waiting at Bright Angel Trail."

EMERY C. KOLB

The Brave Ones

The Journals and Letters of the 1911-1912
Expedition Down the Green and Colorado Rivers by
Ellsworth L. Kolb and Emery C. Kolb
including the journal of Hubert R. Lauzon

transcribed and edited by
William C. Suran

FRETWATER PRESS
2003

The Journals of Ellsworth

Fretwater Press
1000 Grand Canyon Avenue
Flagstaff, Arizona 86001
www.fretwater.com

Printed in Canada
First Edition
06 07 7 6 5 4 3 2

ISBN
(cloth) 1-892327-11-2
(paper) 1-892327-12-0

Library of Congress Control Number: 2003090402
This book was set in Adobe Minion
designed and typeset in Adobe InDesign,
on a Macintosh G4

Front cover photograph:
Emery and Ellsworth Kolb
Walthenberg Rapid, Grand Canyon
Christmas Day 1911
courtesy Emery C. Kolb Collection
Northern Arizona University
Cline Library

to the Grand Canyon Historical Society

Table of Contents

Emery Kolb

BOATING—WHITEWATER BOATING—was still raw when Ellsworth and Emery Kolb launched on their eleven-hundred mile journey in 1911. Major John Wesley Powell and his men had struggled down the Green and Colorado Rivers in 1869 and 1871–72, but had portaged every major rapid they could, and had been abused by those few they ran. They had chosen Whitehall-style lake boats—built to go fast, turn poorly, and withstand tremendous impact. They did all those things. The crew was lucky to have survived. Powell's lectures, articles, and books spread word of the magnificent canyons, the violent river, and of his harrowing adventure.

Twenty years later Frank M. Brown and Robert Brewster Stanton made another well-publicized attempt on the Colorado. They used a similar boat to Powell's—keeled for speed, powered by men rowing with their backs downstream, and aimed by a steersman in the rear with a long sweep oar. Brown and two crewmen drowned on the first voyage. Stanton, with unwavering determination, returned that winter with stronger boats and lifejackets. And although they, too, portaged most of the difficult rapids and were trounced in those they ran, they came out the far end alive.

Yet neither Powell's nor Stanton's high-profile expeditions did much to further whitewater boating. The boats and techniques that the Kolbs emulated, and that are still used today, evolved organically on the upper streams of the Colorado system, and are primarily credited to Nathaniel Galloway, a trapper from Vernal, Utah. Where Galloway's ideas came from are unknown, but by the early 1890s he was building small, shallow-draft, flat-bottomed boats, upturned at either end for ease of pivoting. In whitewater, Galloway turned and pulled upstream, against the current, lowering himself gingerly between rock and wave, ferrying from side to side as the situation dictated.

Galloway was not the only boater between Stanton's day and the Kolbs'—others went down the Green and Colorado too, but most are poorly known. George Flavell built a small boat in Green River, Wyoming, in April 1896 and, with companion Ramón Montéz, spent the next eight-and-one-half months negotiating most every rapid between there and Needles, California. Information on what type of boat he ran, and how he ran it, is hazy. One account states that in flat water he *stood and pushed* his oars—Flavell mentions *pulling* in rapids. Some say he added a *sweep oar* for Montéz—Flavell mentions a *second set of oars* for big water, and admits that careening and good luck were mainstays of his style.

In 1903 Elias "Hum" Woolley rowed some sort of boat through Grand Canyon with two young companions. Almost nothing is known of this trip. Arthur Sanger, who rode along, says little more definitive than, "Only the wonderful river knowledge and oarsmanship of Hum—Woolley saved us from the vortex.... I am scared."

In 1907 riverman Bert Loper teamed with Charles Russell and Edwin Monett to run the Colorado. They purchased three sixteen-foot steel-and-wood boats from Michigan. Photographs of Russell's boat show it to be akin to Powell's, with a keel board running the length of the bottom. Loper's boat and camera were damaged in Cataract Canyon and he lagged behind. Russell and Monett continued into Grand Canyon, losing Monett's boat in the Upper Granite Gorge. Monett straggled aboard Russell's boat and they rowed on. They hiked to the canyon rim to resupply, and there met the Kolb brothers. The Kolbs accompanied them back to the river and photographed them rowing off downstream. Russell and Monett soon lost their remaining boat, but retrieved it downriver and continued on to Needles. Their boating style is indiscernible—but their persistence unquestioned.

By this time, the Kolb brothers were thinking about a river trip of their own. But although they corresponded with Charles Russell, he and his boating failed to gain their allegiance. Nor did the Kolbs turn to Powell, Stanton, Flavell, or Woolley. They looked to Galloway.

In 1909, Galloway launched a four-man expedition financed by Julius F. Stone, a wealthy Ohio businessman who longed for adventure. Galloway supervised the construction of sturdy boats to his specifications, and the men launched from Green River, Wyoming, on September 12 with Stone an eager student at the oars of one boat. Galloway instructed well apparently, though on occasion, to the other boatmen's chagrin, he elected to take all three boats through some of the more difficult rapids. On November 3 the men climbed the Bright Angel Trail to Grand Canyon Village. Although they do not mention having met the Kolbs, the village was too small and tight for them not to have. Stone and Galloway completed their expedition without serious incident, and the Kolbs began correspondence with both men. Stone sent them blueprints and specifications for boats and gear.

In his 1914 book, *Through the Grand Canyon from Wyoming to Mexico*, Ellsworth explains the origin of their boating style, "As to this method, unused as yet by either of us, we had received careful verbal instructions from Mr. Stone, who had made the trip two years before our own venture; and from other friends of Nathan Galloway, the trapper, the man who first introduced the method on the Green and Colorado rivers.... He it is who has worked out the type of boats we used, and their management in the dangerous waters of the Colorado."

Galloway toyed with the idea of accompanying the Kolb brothers. He might have, but for one thing. Ellsworth explains in his book: "It was suggested, also, that we might secure the help of some one of the voyagers who had been members of one of the previous expeditions. But—we may as well be frank about it—we did not wish to be piloted through the Colorado by a guide. We wanted to make our own trip in our own way. If we failed, we would have no one but ourselves to blame; if we succeeded, we would have all the satisfaction that comes from original, personal exploration."

So off the Kolbs went, with full benefit of Galloway's boats and methods, but with not a moment of hands-on practice or guidance. Their tale reflects the rawness of their skills. Their calamities in the Canyon of Lodore, in Marble Canyon at Soap Creek Rapid, and at Walthenberg Rapid deep in the heart of Grand Canyon on Christmas Eve, might all have been avoided with the sober experience of Galloway in charge. Yet lost, too, would have been the magic of the Kolbs' tale. Ellsworth was right.

The Kolbs' book, and their movies and lectures, shown at their rimside studio for the next sixty years, overhauled the world of whitewater boating. In place of the formidable canyon and lethal river portrayed by previous expeditions, the Kolbs brought forth a grand adventure that two everyman brothers could tackle and come out alive and grinning. Ellsworth's book became a river guide to many who followed. With that book and the brothers' film—still the longest-running movie anywhere—the Kolbs cemented the Galloway style of rapid-water navigation, and eased its transition to the increasingly popular pastime that rafting has become today, nearly a century later.

ELLSWORTH KOLB died in 1960, Emery in 1976 at the age of 95. The Emery C. Kolb Collection went to Northern Arizona University Cline Library, where initial processing began. Funds failed and the collection languished for several years. Then in the late 1980s Bill Suran spent three years as a volunteer helping to process the vast collection—tens of thousands of negatives and photographs, and veritable mountains of paperwork—correspondence, notes, and every receipt the Kolb brothers had ever laid hands on. In the course of shoveling, sorting, and shelving, Suran stumbled across the original Kolb diaries. He was fascinated. "No one had ever transcribed them," he recalls, "They were just layin' around there loose." Suran photocopied them: Emery's and Ellsworth's handsome leather-bound loose-leaf notebooks, and one supplemental stitched notebook of Ellsworth's.

Suran spent more than a year transcribing them in the evenings and weekends at home with his wife Sibyl. Emery's journal was in good shape and not too difficult to decipher. Ellsworth, however, had at one point used a water-soluble pen that ran when the journal was doused, and in another section used some sort of indelible pencil that smudged against the writing on the facing page, all but obliterating anything legible. For months Suran stared and studied, squinting at times through a magnifying glass, and wrested the words printed here. As well, Suran read the many letters between the Kolbs and others—before, during, and after the 1911 trip— and has included much of this critical material in the narrative.

Suran also tracked down Pat Lauzon, Bert's son, in Ash Fork, Arizona, and obtained a photocopy of Bert's typewritten transcription of his journal. This Suran re-transcribed, interleaving it with the Kolb journals to round out the story of the last wild leg of their journey.

Beginning in 1989, for nearly a decade, Suran solicited publishers to no avail. Meanwhile, he wrote *With the Wings of an Angel: A Biography of Ellsworth and Emery Kolb, Photographers of Grand Canyon*. This, too, failed to interest publishers, so Suran released it on the internet, where it can still be downloaded from the Grand Canyon Historical Society's website. In 1991, with the cooperation of the Grand Canyon Natural History Association, Suran produced a small book: *The Kolb Brothers of Grand Canyon: Being a Collection of Tales of High Adventure, Memorable Incidents, & Humorous Anecdotes*. In the mean time, Suran remains a stalwart volunteer with Grand Canyon Historical Society, and assembles their regular publication of canyon history, *The Ol' Pioneer.*

Now, finally, after these journals have languished into a new millennium—ninety-one years after three exhausted, banged, bruised, and often more than a little damp men scrawled them on the riverbank—comes their on-the-spot rendition of the Kolb Expedition. In final preparation for publication, with the unstinting aid of my wife Jeri Ledbetter, I crosschecked Suran's work against the original diaries (finding precious few errors) and can attest to its accuracy. In the intervening years since Suran's work, the Lauzon family donated Bert's original handwritten diaries to Cline Library—one version with just a few cryptic and often illegible notes per day, and a second with Lauzon's thoughts filled in. We have amended the Lauzon transcription to conform to this second handwritten version.

It is both a pleasure and an honor to present this long overdue volume to the historians, river-runners, and adventure fans of the West. We owe a great debt to the brothers Kolb and Bert Lauzon for recording their tales. We owe an equal debt to Bill Suran for rescuing them from musty obscurity and breathing them back to life.

BRAD DIMOCK
January, 2003

Ellsworth Kolb's journal, right

Emery Kolb's journal, below

introduction

ELLSWORTH L. "ED" KOLB drifted west from his birthplace of Pittsburgh, Pennsylvania, and arrived at the South Rim of Grand Canyon in 1901. The next year his brother Emery C. Kolb, five years younger, followed. The brothers bought a small photography business in Williams, Arizona, and in 1903 moved it to a tent at the head of Bright Angel Trail. They soon replaced the tent with a small wooden studio, which they remodeled and expanded for many years until it contained comfortable living quarters, a photography studio, a gift shop, and an auditorium. In 1905 Emery married Blanche Bender who, in 1908, gave birth to Edith Kolb. In 1911, Ellsworth, 36, and Emery, 31, launched their expedition down the Green and Colorado River. A third brother, Ernest V. Kolb, came out from Pittsburgh to run the studio in their absence, and joined his brothers for a short stretch of the river trip.

Ellsworth and Emery Kolb spent just over one hundred days on the river between Green River, Wyoming, and Needles, California, pausing midway for a month at their rimside studio. During that voyage they kept extensive journals, chronicling each day's activities and mishaps, and telling of characters they met along the way. Ellsworth returned to Needles in May 1913, bought a small boat from a Mojave Indian for eighteen dollars, and completed his voyage to the mouth of the Colorado. Although no journal exists for this portion of the trip, Ellsworth tells of it in his 1914 book, *Through the Grand Canyon from Wyoming to Mexico.*

❧ ❧ ❧

BEGINNING WITH John Wesley Powell's first trip through the canyons of the Green and the Colorado Rivers, many of those daring men who tackled the hazardous journey kept records of their exploits along the way. Powell compiled his notes in 1875, years after he made his two trips. Although he virtually ignored the second expedition, seventeen-year-old Frederick F. Dellenbaugh, who accompanied Powell on the second trip, recorded it in *A Canyon Voyage*, in 1908. For years this book was the guide for other river travelers.

The Brown and Stanton expeditions of 1889–90 were recorded in detail and published in *Scribner's* magazine and elsewhere. George Flavell kept a journal of his 1896–97 trip, as did and Julius Stone on his 1896–97 trip with Nathaniel Galloway. All of these accounts have now been published and the original works preserved in the archives of various libraries. The journals of Ellsworth and Emery Kolb, now housed in the Northern Arizona University Cline Library, have never been published, and due to their fragile condition few have had the privilege of viewing them.

The journals were written in small, pocket-sized, looseleaf note-books in pencil, sometimes so faint as to be nearly impossible to read, sometimes with a soft lead pencil which has smudged beyond legibility. Ellsworth on one occasion wrote with a soluble pencil; a dunking in the river causing the writing to run. These problems along with individual handwriting, sometimes large and clear, other times small and tightly scribbled, possibly showing the nervousness or even fear over what lay ahead, added to the problems of transcribing the records.

The Kolbs throughout the trip kept separate journals, each record-ing his own thoughts of the day's travel. Hubert R. Lauzon, who joined the party midway through Grand Canyon, kept a journal as well. While not a part of the Kolb Collection, I include it to give as full a picture of the expedition as possible. The three journals are presented together on a day-to-day basis, so the reader may follow the trip with ease.

For convenience I have also included the letters found in the collec-tion pertaining to the trip as well as newspaper items published in the *Coconino Sun*, the Flagstaff paper at the time. I have copied the text with spelling and punctuation as it appears. All words marked through or crossed out in the original are indicated ~~thusly~~. Words and com-ments in square brackets are mine, added occasionally for clarity.

William C. Suran
Tuesday, October 24, 1989

The Brave Ones

THE KOLB BROTHERS made their living as photographers. The images they captured reflect this. The Emery C. Kolb Collection contains over eighty thousand photographs and negatives. For this volume we have chosen more than two dozen images, most of which have rarely, if ever, been published.

We have included several stereo images. They are printed as they came out of the camera, which is, oddly, with the left-eye view on the right-hand side and vice versa. This is convenient, however, for the technique called *cross-eyed freeviewing*. If you care to try it, stare at a stereo image and cross your eyes slightly until you see three images. The middle one will be three-dimensional. This technique takes practice and rest, but is startlingly effective once you get the hang of it. An internet search of *cross-eyed freeviewing* will bring up many helpful methods for learning the technique.

All photographs are printed courtesy of Northern Arizona University Cline Library and Emery Lehnert. The call numbers for these images are listed on page 170.

Running Tapeats Creek Rapid. Bert Lauzon standing by.

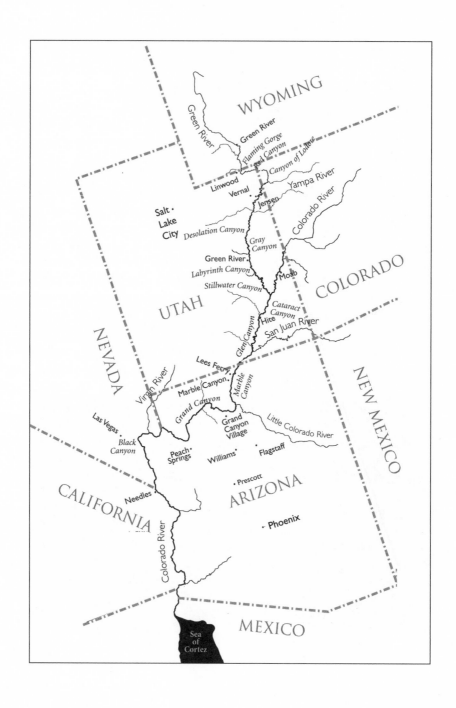

part one

The Preparation

THERE IS NO RECORD indicating when the Kolb brothers came upon the idea of duplicating Major John Wesley Powell's voyage of 1869 through the canyons of the Green and Colorado Rivers. Emery Kolb related in his later years the idea was his brother's. The first evidence they planned such a trip appears in a letter from Charles S. Russell[1] dated 17 March 1908:

> ...I should be greatly interested in such a trip as you contemplate, and should you succeed you would be the first parties to secure a continuous series of good photographs of the canyon. I should like very much to talk the matter over with you as I think I could give you some valuable pointers that would be worth your while. Let me hear from you again.

The Kolbs knew they could add nothing scientifically to such an excursion through the canyons, and both felt it would be folly to risk their lives in such turbulent waters just for the fun of it. As their business was photography they planned to make the first moving pictures of the trip with the newly invented motion picture machine. Such thoughts were in their minds as early as the spring of 1910 when they wrote letters seeking a motion picture camera. They received a reply from one addressed to The R & S Film and Supply Co. of Kansas City, Missouri on 3 June 1910:

> ...As to the machine for taking motion pictures (Cinematograph) will say these machines cost $250.00; either Powers or Selig...

The Fireproof Film Co. of Rochester, New York, sent Kolb Brothers the name and address of a paper published for independent operators of motion picture cameras, in a letter dated 25 June 1910:

> Answering your favor of June 17th, would say that we herewith give you the name of the newspaper that is published for the independents. The name of the publication is the "Moving Picture News" published by the Cinematograph Publishing Company, 30 West 13th Street, New York City.
>
> In this publication you can find all the information you desire, and it gives the addresses of all independent makers of film...

On 29 July the same year, The Edison Manufacturing Co. of Orange, New Jersey, wrote:

> ...For Motion Picture Cameras, we would advise you that these are only supplied for the manufacturer's use and further information concerning them may be obtained through the Motion Picture Patents Company N.Y.C. In this connection, however, permit us to state that we take special motion pictures, and will be pleased to submit an estimate at your request. These pictures can be made up from negatives which will remain your property, and positive prints supplied from time to time, as you may need them...

A second letter from Edison Manufacturing Company dated 16 September 1910 restates the fact that the cameras are supplied for manufacturer's use only but adds:

> ...We regret that our proposition as to taking of pictures for you does not prove entertaining...

It is certain the Edison Company was unfamiliar with the scope of the work the Kolbs had in mind as well as the environment in which the proposed film was to be made.

The Lumiere Company, New York City wrote on 20 November:

> We beg to acknowledge receipt of your esteemed favor of the 4th inst. In reply beg to state that we can supply you a Lumiere Moving Picture taking camera at a price of $450.00 F.O.B. New York, duty paid... It is one of the most compact moving picture cameras on the market, and is so solid that it obviates entirely the trouble usually caused by vibration. The magazines on this instrument can be changed more rapidly than on any other moving picture camera made...

While undecided and still looking for the camera Ellsworth turned his attention to other aspects of the planned trip. He studied Powell's book *The Colorado River and its Canyons* describing the perils of his first voyage through the unknown, and to Frederick Dellenbaugh's account of Powell's second trip in *A Canyon Voyage*. Although there is no reference to correspondence with Robert Brewster Stanton, it is certain Ellsworth received information pertaining to his trips of 1889 and 1890. He then sought first hand information from Julius Stone, a wealthy business man from Ohio, who made the trip from Green River, Wyoming to Needles, California for the adventure of it in 1909. A letter dated 20 April 1911 from Julius Stone indicates their plans were beginning to formulate:

> ...The address, for which you inquire, is The Metropolitan Air Goods Company, Reading, Massachusetts, and I am quite sure if you remind them of the camp beds they made for me a couple of years ago you will get exactly what you require; if I had it to do over again I wouldn't change that part of our equipment at all...

Their search for the camera became more complicated as time passed. The Kolbs wrote to Frederick I. Monsen, an agent in New York City, requesting he locate the equipment. Monsen replied on 7 May 1911:

Since I last wrote you I have looked into the matter of cameras and can find absolutely nothing for sale or rent. Fact is cameras are picked up as soon as offered for sale as the Motion Trust people do not want any cameras on the market. It is impossible now to buy a camera from the makers in Europe and have it shipped here. The Motion Trust people have stopped all that but as we no longer live in a free country there is nothing to do about it...

Now, not being able to buy or rent you a camera, here is a chance for you if you wish to take it up. I own two cameras and never use more than one. I'll sell (not rent) you either of these instruments at less than it cost me. They are both new instruments and are in perfect working order, so perfect I do not care which one I retain for my own purpose. The larger instrument is a Pathe and the magazine holds 300 feet of film. It is complete with every modern device and there is nothing better made. There are 5 or 6 magazines and panorama tripod, cases, etc, etc,. With this is a Printing Outfit which cost me $125 and with it you can turn out as fine work as the best of the factories. I also have other things that go with the outfit for which I would make no charge. This outfit taking camera and printing camera, magazines, tripod, panorama tripod head, and carrying cases, cost me $400, you may have it for $250. The other outfit is a smaller camera holding 100 feet of film but equal in the quality of its work (see sample enclosed) to the more expensive machine. I will sell this camera with the above described printing outfit for $175, it cost me $250. This is an Urban Machine fitted with genuine Zeiss lens and, on account of its light weight, very valuable to me in the field.

This is only a suggestion for you to consider. You can write to Mr. W.B. Cline, Eastman Kodak Co., Rochester, N.Y. who knows both instruments and will be glad to give you any information. Mr. Cline is Eastman's expert on Motion Photography. Any other information I can give you on this or any other subject will give me pleasure. With best wishes for your success, I am...

On 12 May 1911 Ellsworth replied:

We wish to thank you for the kind treatment you have shown us in regards to the motion picture camera. The younger brother Emery C. Kolb will be in New York about May 25th. or 26th. and we hope to find you in that vicinity and will take up the matter personally.

We note that you say nothing about perforated films and we have been given the impression that it is very difficult to get this. No doubt you can help us in this matter also.

We have had a very good season here and have been making the most of it.

Thanking you once more for the kind consideration you have shown us and with best wishes, we are

After writing this letter plans at Grand Canyon changed and Ellsworth rather than Emery made the trip to New York. Preparations were now carried out from the East Coast and the Canyon, Emery continuing with the business at the studio. Things began to move forward rapidly. In May an article appeared in the San Francisco, California, newspaper regarding the upcoming trip and initiated a letter from E. A. Evans of that city, on 26 May that read:

Understanding from the inclosed clipping you intend to take a canyon trip, I take this liberty to write.

Presuming you may need a larger crew, I wish to state that I would like to fill in, I would be willing to give my services gratis, as that trip appeals to me.

Am California born, 30 years of age, weigh 152 lbs, 5 ft 7 in, unmarried.

I have been through the mill, as I have been in the army, in the Philippines in '98, have worked on the sea, mining, timber, ranch, railroader, farm and city, in fact I have knocked around considerable. I know I can stand the gaft. You might call me an old timer.

I have taken a small trip of 500 miles down the Missouri in a small skiff, but I know it does not compare with your intended trip.

I know your trip is going to be a little tough, as I have read a great deal of some of the canyon trips. F. Dellenbaugh's 'A Canyon Voyage' and Major Powell's first trip. G. W. Jame's 'The grand canyon of Arizona' R. Staton's trip of the first and second expedition, when Mr.

Brown lost out below Soap Creek, also of Hanborough and Richards losing out below Knab Wash, and also of that pretty tough spot at Diamond Creek.

I know it will be hard graft, and lots of it, and I am more than willing to take the trip, if I could kick in with the outfit, knowing full well that I will have to go some.

I just gave some brief facts, but if you should care to answer, I will give you more details, I only want to know if I can go along.

Hoping you will consider this seriously, and let me know in the near future.

A letter of 29 June from Julius Stone indicates further correspondence seeking information on construction of boats. Stone replied:

Dear Boys:-

Under a separate cover I am sending you a blue print of the boats we had, showing their construction in detail, excepting that the skag was removable by reason of its having been attached by two through bolts, so that when we came to relatively quiescent water, such as from Green River, Wyo. to the mouth of Sheep Creek and from the mouth of Gray Canyon to the head waters of the Colorado, also through Glen Canyon and below the mouth of Grand Canyon, we could have the benefit of the skags in position in order to keep the boats from swaying, thereby making it very much easier to cover the intervening distance, while during the more turbulent canyons we went without the skags, having unfastened them and taking them into the boats.

I will send you the specifications for the construction of the boats, in a separate letter as soon as I get back to the Bank, so that you may know just what material was used. I also am sending you a copy of the government maps covering the entire course of the river as far as published, showing wherever we camped. You will note that these maps go no farther north than the Wyoming boundary line and no farther east than the Colorado line, therefore, that portion of Green River north of Utah, covering our camps No. 1, 2 and 3, and east of Utah, covering camps No. 9 to 12 inclusive, is not shown.

The bend of the river out into Colorado just about takes in Lodore

Canyon, which is the wildest and most difficult of all the canyons north of Cataract.

Our boats were constructed by The Pouliot Boat Co. of Detroit, Mich.

Please let me know if the maps reach you in good order, and about when you expect to start. I am preparing excerpts from my notes taken of the trip so far as they appertain to the method of passing down such various rapids as we could not run, and will send you these prior to the time you start, or else bring them to you, as it is possible that I may attend the meeting of the Society for Solar Research in Pasadena during the first week in September...

The specifications of Julius Stone's boat were as follows:

GENERAL DIMENSIONS.
Length over all 16 ft. 4 inches.
Beam 46″ outside.
Depth 18 inches.
Boats to be built of clear white pine for sides and bottoms ⅝″ thick.
Decks and bulk heads and seats to be of clear white pine.
Frames to be of clear hard elm ¾ in. by 1 in.
Bottom stringers to be of clear white oak in one length 1½ in. x 2 in. as shown on plans.
Gunwales for sides to be of clear white oak in one length 1½ in. x 1½ in. as shown on plans.
Stems to be of clear white oak 2½ in. thick as shown on plans.
Sterns to be of clear white pine 1 in. thick and re-inforced with white oak.
Forward and after hatches to be as shown on plans, with hinges, and canvas covered with 8 oz. duck.
All planking to be copper nailed and burred and riveted.
All screws to be of brass and all bolts to be galvanized iron.
Stem irons to be ¾ in. half round and well screwed into place.
Finish to be three coats of lead color paint inside and out.
All work to be done the same as agreed by Mr. Gallaway and Mr. Pouliot.

Center ridge pole to be clear white pine as shown on plans.

Each boat to be fitted with three 8 ft. white ash oars and one pair of oarlocks.

All materials which enter into the construction of these boats to be first class of their respective kind, and labor performed in a neat, thorough and workmanlike manner in accordance with the true intent of these plans and specifications.

Using the information received from Stone, the Kolbs prepared plans and forwarded them to the Racine Boat and Engine Company in Racine, Wisconsin, who returned a proposal for constructing "Two Special Row Boats" according to the specifications on 16 June as follows: [*note the difference in materials requested by the Kolbs.*]

DIMENSIONS. Length 16-ft. 4-in. Beam 48-in. Model as per blue print submitted.

FRAMEWORK. Ribs and deck frames to be made from clear white oak of the proper dimensions, spaced 9″ center. Bottom planking to be of clear white cedar, ⅝″ in thickness, carvel construction. Side plank to be same material ½″ in thickness, lap straked, to be fastened to the ribs with brass screws, and ~~two~~ three copper rivets between each rib. Bottom planks to have an oak strip over each joint ⅜″ in thickness x 2″ wide, well riveted to the boat.

JOINER WORK. Gunwales to be made from cypress 1¼″ x 2½ well riveted to the boat. Forward deck to be 6-ft. 6-in. long, fitted with water tight hatch of a suitable size. Decks to be covered with ⅜″ white cedar, covered with heavy canvas, cemented on, tacked at the edges. Hatch to be fitted with suitable frame, extending above the deck 1″ and made perfectly water tight, fitted with hatch cover, made from ⅝″ white cedar, covered with canvas, and to be fastened to the hatch with three thumb bolts on each side. After decks will be 5-ft. 6-in. long, constructed the same as the forward deck. Bulkheads at the end of decks made from ⅝″ white cedar, and to be perfectly water tight. The extreme forward and after end will be fitted with galvanized air tanks. ½″ iron bolt arranged on stern for carrying.

Ellsworth Kolb at the Racine Boat Company

COCKPIT will be arranged as shown on blue print, to have one cross seat. Coaming at the forward and after deck, to extend above the deck 4″ and finish off at the side.

FINISH. Boat to be given three coats of white lead paint inside and outside, of a lead color, and trimmed with dark trimmings. All seams to be filled with elastic seam composition.

FITTINGS consist of iron stem band; removable skeg in the after end of boat; two pair of 8-foot ash oars, with special tips; one pair of galvanized oar locks and sockets. Forward compartment of boat to be lined with light galvanized iron, made perfectly watertight.

The company proposed to completed the work on the two boats about July 25 for the sum of $450. The terms were fifty percent of the cost to accompany the order, the balance to be paid when the boats were ready to ship. The delivery to be F.O.B. cars Racine, Wisconsin. The proposal was accepted and signed by E. C. Kolb, with no date indicated but it must have been accepted promptly.

Both brothers agreed it would be wise to have a third man accompany them to aid in taking pictures and to serve as helper. Emery began the search and offered the job to a Reese B. Griffith. On 10 July, an agreement was drawn up between Griffith and Kolb Brothers which read:

Agreement between Reese B. Griffith and Kolb Bros.

Reese B. Griffith hereby offers his service to Kolb Bros. on there proposed trip down the Colorado River on the following terms.

1. That he is to row one boat as long as their is one boat for each and every person in the party but shall give up his boat, on request in case of accident to any other boat. That he is to have charge of the camp cooking and to be general helper and at all times to be under the direction and command of Kolb Bros. to any reasonable extent and at all times will accept his share in any work or difficulty which they may encounter, to the best of his ability.

2. Reese B. Griffith hereby releases Kolb Bros. from any responsibility or any liability for any accident or injuries, serious or trivial which might occur and takes all risks entirely on his own responsibility.

3. That he shall not take any photos for his own use with any camera larger than a no. 3A. Eastman Kodak and only on condition that Kolb Bros. shall supply the original negative film and shall retain ownership of said films after development allowing R. B. Griffith any prints he shall wish for his own immediate use but in no case to furnish sell or barter the photos to any publication, lecturer or private [indivi]dual without the full consent of Kolb Bros. All photos of any par[ticular] value will be copyrighted by Kolb Bros. Reese B. Griffith [un]derstands said Kolb Bros will not have any one in the[ir employ...] who is interested in making photos for commercial purpo[ses ...] not permit this privilege to interfere with his duties. Kolb Bros. to be allowed to regulate the weight...

4. Kolb Bros. are to be allowed to regulate the weight of baggage wi[th]in a reasonable limit.

5. Reese B. Griffith will supply his own personal wearing apparel an[d] bedding excepting a mattress which shall be supplied by

Kolb Bros. All other actual necessities are to be supplied by Kolb Bros.

6. For the above services Kolb Bros. agree to pay Reese B. Griffith $25.00 to apply on travel expenses to Green River, Wyo. and a similar amount at Needles, Calif. in case he finishes the trip that far or farther. Kolb Bros. also agree to pay R. B. Griffith at the rate of $100.00 Dollars per. month and board except in case of any continued delay in one place when he shall be paid at the rate of $2.00 per day and board.

7. In case of sickness, dissatisfaction or any reason whatsoever either party shall have the privilege of terminating this contract by giving three days notice and in no case bind themselves to conti[nue] it against their will.

The terms of the contract apparently were not to Griffith's liking. Whether or not he signed it is unknown. No further mention is made of him.

The Racine Boat Company acknowledged receipt of the Kolbs' check for the initial payment for the boats in a letter dated 17 July:

Gentlemen:-

We have your favor of the 8th inst. enclosing your check for $200.00, which has been placed to your credit.

We induced the postal authorities here to deliver to us your letter addressed to the Racine Boat and Engine Co., and find therein your check for $175.00, which we are returning herewith as you have requested.

Kindly acknowledge receipt of this letter, and oblige,

On 4 August Emery received a letter mailed in Vernal, Utah, from another party interested in making the trip:

Mr. ~~E. C.~~ Colb Bros.

Dear Sir

I have been informed by Mr. D.D. Rust[2] that you are Contemplating a trip through the Canyons including the Grand Canyon for the purpose of getting mooveing pictures & etc.

I am quite anctious to Hear from you & learn something of your plans & etc. & the number of boats & people that you expect in your party.

I am very much interested as I was planning a similar trip for last fall, but finely Desided to drop it; at the request of a friend.

I am expecting to make a boating trip through the Canyons of Green River this fawl.

Please let me hear from you to give me dates & the point of your Starting.

Very Truly,
Nathan Galloway[3]

Ellsworth wrote Emery from New York City 8 August regarding the materials purchased for the trip:

...I went to D Abercrombies and got some oarlocks like Stones. The factory did not have that kind.

Mr.. Stone wants to send us a hydrometer and barometer and take certain readings for him. Lodore Canyon for instance. His only recorded 6000 ft. and that was not high enough. He offered me his set of lenses, interchangable, but said nothing about camera. He also offered me Powell's book if I would bring it back but I declined. I have tried to get it but have not been successful...

Don't forget this. The middle section of boat will be shipped to the Canyon unless you order different so suit yourself but act quickly if you wish order changed. I think two boats would be enough and we could use the tin boat when we got there if we needed it.

I suppose Reed's partner is going. How about it and on what terms?

The hardest thing to get seems to be a water tight box. The only thing I can find so far seems to be an English box for army officers that has kept papers dry 6 years under water 30 x 15 x 14 in. $22.00. I think we should have one for M.P. camera if nothing else shows up.

I will keep you posted on purchases. Don't let money get behind in bank when your six months expire place it on check and let me know...

Another letter addressed to Emery on August 10 indicated his feelings toward Galloway's desire to accompany them on the trip:

> ...I suppose Rust & G [Galloway] still insist on G. going and you are telling R we may start at Green River, Utah if boats are delayed too long so-as to throw him off. I don't want G to row my boat, otherwise I stand for any arrangement you make concerning a third man. We will hardly get the pictures we want without one...

Emery received a letter on 14 August 1911 from H.E. Foster of the Southern Pacific Company, who knew Emery from Grand Canyon:

> I arrived in the city early this morning to again take up my duties with the Company and shortly after noon time Mr. Evans called at my office for interview, presenting telegram sent by you. I handed him the letter you had written explaining nature of your trip and what would be expected of the man that went along. Also talked in detail with him and explained matters to him about as you directed that I should. I believe he understands thoroughly about what will be required of him. He stated that he did not own a camera and that he did not know anything about their operation and that his intention was to make the trip strictly for the novelty of the experience. He appears to be a man of a roving disposition and confirmed in words the statements made to you by letter about his army experience, travels and books that he has read about Powell's trip through the Canyon country. He looks about 30 or 35 years of age, medium height, medium light hair and appears to be a man that is used to roughing it, which he admitted. From his appearance I should not take him for a drinking man nor a slouch and looks to be a cleanly sort of person. I explained to him just about what you would require of him and he stated that he would be very glad to accept your proposition and would take things as they came without complaining. I told him you wanted a man that would make himself agreeable generally and he said he thought he could fill the bill on that score as he always tried to adapt himself to whatever conditions might be presented. In order to preclude the possibility of his thinking

that men were hard to get for this job I told him that you had had several applications but would consider his application favorably should his references prove satisfactory. He gave me the names of several persons located in this city whom I endeavored to reach by telephone after he had departed. I was successful this afternoon in reaching one of them, a Mr. Levy, clerk in Judge Van Nostrands Court (Superior Court) who states: "He is a very good man and I can personally vouch for his honesty. I knew him well when he was employed as an extra carrier in the post office department and found him all right. If he does not turn out all right you can come back at me." He gave two other references, a Mr. Gallagher, who is employed in the office of the Postmaster at San Francisco, and a Mr. McCarthy, who is employed in the County Treasurer's office. I rang up both these people but they were not in their office at the time. I also rang up their residences and found that they were employed as stated and can probably reach them tomorrow by telephone. After talking with them I will write you again as to what they have to say about Evans. Thought I would get this letter off tonight as you are no doubt limited in time and want to get the matter settled as shortly as possible.

Evans appears to be very anxious to go with you on the trip and is all enthused with having such a novel experience, and promises to abide by whatever instructions are given him, to do all the camp work and heavy work in general. I made it clear to him that you were "the boss of the job," that he was not to be considered in any way running the expedition but was to do most of the real hard work connected therewith.

I trust the above report will be satisfactory to you and that your expedition will meet with every success. If I can be of further assistance in any way I will gladly do what I can for you. Drop me a line from time to time if there is any information you will need that I can furnish.

The Racine Boat Company wrote Ellsworth in Pittsburgh, Pennsylvania, on 15 August:

Replying to your favor of 11th inst. the two large boats are all ready to be shipped, and would have been shipped yesterday had we not received your letter.

As we noticed you have bought some special oar locks which you wish to install in the boat, We are holding the boats awaiting the oar locks and will ship them out as soon as they arrive.

We are enclosing you herewith, a bill for the two large boats, amounting to $452.00 with a credit of $250.00 leaving a balance of $202.00. Also a bill for the center section which amounts to $28.00, two pair of 7-foot ash oars $5.00, and one pair of oar locks and sockets $.50, or a total $33.50, together with the $202.00 leaves a balance of $235.50.

If we do not hear from you before the boats are shipped, we will draw on you for the $235.50, and ship the boat as directed.

The center section will probably go forward a day or two later.

Hoping this is satisfactory, we are

An invoice was enclosed with the letter.

Emery sent a telegram to E. A. Evans 14 August indicating the selection of a third man to accompany them on the trip was still open. Evans replied on 15 August:

Received your telegram and called on Mr. Foster yesterday.

He explained quite thoroughly the kind of work you intend to do, and what would be required of me.

I gave him a number of high class references regarding my character, which will convince him that I am conscientious sober and industrious.

I have been invited to go on several camping and boating trips because of my congeniality together with my ability as a cook, and have absolutely no fear of your being the least bit disappointed along these lines.

Awaiting further orders regarding detail of the trip, I am

Ellsworth wrote Emery from New York in an undated letter:

…Next, I spent a full day with D Abercrombies and am glad I went there instead of A. &. T. Prices are quite different and he is a good fellow. I went over things quite thoroughly and he is to figure the whole thing out then we will eliminate what we can do without. I have no idea what that bill will be but you had better take a good breath. I am getting a dark room 4½ x 6 x 7 ft high to go inside tent $17.00 not bad when you think what you pay for a changing bag. They are making a tent regular shape 8 x 9¾ x 3 ft wall to be put up with 2 oars, no poles. It is green, and lighter and softer than Tanilite. He invented both. I have not got rubber beds or life preservers yet. Have been busy every minute.

Have just been out to see Munson [Frederick Monsen]. His father died two days ago and he was just leaving. I will see him Sat. eve & Sunday. He will get films. He says those films are all right as far as perforation goes. That is #5 Schneider and the only thing is you must have the same positive perforation. I have not been to see Genert or Photo Cines yet. What I meant about shipping them from Chi. was that the fellow there said he merely acted for accommodation but he wrote explaining the matter and I shipped them here.

Now here is where finances stand.

About $500 in bank	Check to C.A	400.00
Your <u>1000</u> Aug 16th	" Abercrombie	50.00
Cash $1500	Check to be given C.A. Co.	600.00
	M.P. Films	$250.00
Possible cost of Abercrombies list, Plates, small films etc.		<u>450.00</u>
1750.00		
Balance on boat about		<u>250.00</u>
		2000.00
		<u>1500.00</u>
Bal. to be placed in bank from receipts.		500.00

This will not include 90 day note for 1300 to
Campbell if I can swing it…
P.S. I will not get a third air mattress. Remember that.

Another letter sent to Emery on 18 August read:

> Boats go today mid section shipped to G.C. a few days ago. I will send check in full so if they draw on Williams bank don't honor check. Negatives just at hand. Had a most satisfactory trip to Boston. The things have to be made to order but I'm sure we are in good hands. Practically everything at cost. He wants good pictures of things in use. Price is on Q.T. I am going to have him get 2 pr. army blankets at 7.50 each 1 for each bed. You can bring 1 extra for yourself. If you wish mattress for other man order to Met. Air Goods Co. to ship to G.R. [Green River, Wyoming] I can get all baggage in the two large bags, with lock will ship as baggage…
>
> Have examined shutter & find Thornton Pickard most simple for 8x10. Will order through Denver. Also will order all films through them. Think I will get focal plane on 5x7. Will go to Rochester in two days. from there home.
>
> Don't reship steel boat. We can carry one passenger. In bad water one man can be on shore most of the time. That would be my opinion at least…
>
> Where some of our money is going.
>
> | | |
> |---|---:|
> | Racine Co. | 485.50 |
> | Steel Boat and frt. | 50.00 |
> | Bot. Here | 315.00 |
> | M.P. Camera | 250.00 |
> | M.P. Films | 250.00 |
> | Other films and plates | 250.00 |
> | Fare | <u>350.00</u> |
> | | 1950.50 |
>
> About $3000 I would say will cover not including finishing films.

Also on the same date Ellsworth included a complete list of material purchased from Abercrombie:

2 Gun cleaners	1.50
2 doz. Fish hooks.	.50
2 steel rods	5.00

2 reels.	3.20
2 lines, 100 yds in all (set fish.)	1.80
2 lines for poles.	1.30
4 oar locks.	7.00
1 Cake turner	.10
1 large grate.	.85
2 locks and chains for bags.	2.00
1 set legs for table.	1.25
2 large duffle bags. (hold all baggage)	5.50
1 alcohol stove	2.50
1 doz. tent pins.	.75
1 Wall pocket.	1.50
1 F. basin	.50
2 folding buckets	1.50
3 Iron camp stools	1.80
1 table top.	2.50
3 W.P. match boxes	1.20
1 Camp " "	1.05
1 Hanging shelves	1.50
1 Comb. Tool kit.	2.00
1 Small broiler	.50
1 Camp pack	5.50
1 Pack harness	2.50
1 Money belt. (E.L.K.)	.75
3 Pocket filters	3.00
1 small ax and sheath	1.40
1 Wall tent 8x9¾ x 3ft wall	31.60
1 W. Pf. tent bag.	1.20
2 Spec flour bags 9 x 30	.80
Including other side	94.80
1½ doz. large safety pins	.48
2 Folding candle lanterns.	5.00
2½ doz. large candles.	1.00
1 Baker Reflector.	3.50
6 Boxes Fly dope.	1.50

1 Sharpening stone.	1.00
1 Cook outfit for 3 (Aluminum)	11.00
2 large fry pans instead of 1 small.	1.75
1 set pans	1.90
1 Cook knife and fork	.80
2　〃　spoons.	.60
1 mop.	.10
3 Dish towles	.45
2 Helmets	2.00
1 Water carrying bottle 2 gal (Canvas)	1.00
3 Boxes flash matches	1.15
1 Swiss Canteen. (alum.)	2.50
1 Compass	5.60
1 Barlow knife	.45
½ doz. 10 lb. food bags waxed fine for exposed films, plates.	.65
1 Pr. shoes. (E.L.K.)	5.50
1 Thermometer.	2.00
2 Boxes screw caulks.	1.00
6 Box Amberoid glue	1.50
1 doz small food bags.	1.00
4 10 lb food bags.	--.----
2 pork bags.	.45
2 Black Rubber ~~Cases~~ Shirts	12.00
2 water proof cases for M.P. Camera, films etc.	35.00
Food samples.	.84
4 over all food bags.	.45
2 Medicine Cases. (First aid)	6.00
1 Dark room.	17.00
2 bags for plate holders.	1.50
	132.57
	94.80
Total Abercrombie	$227.37

----

2 sponges.	1.00
2 Thermos bottles & case	4.25
1 roll. adhesive tape	.50

Bot elsewhere	5.75

- -

Metropolitan air goods Co give us confidential dis.	
Want photos of beds in use. 30% dis.	
2 Sleeping bags @ 25.00	50.00
2 Utility cushions (Collars)	6.00
3 2-qt hot water bottles	<u>6.00</u>
	62.00
30% dis. conditional	18.60
	43.40
3 life jacket life preservers (cost)	9.00
3 Waterproof carrying bags (10.00)	30.00
	82.40

- -

	5.75
	227.35
Total outside of boats & books telegrams.	315.52

A final letter from New York on 20 August 1911 was mailed to Emery:

> I leave here tomorrow night ~~from~~ for Rochester. Home Wed...
> I got 8 doz. of the 5x7 Imperial Plates. The English strike has tied things up. I am getting 12 doz (1 case) 8x10 and have ordered 3 cases 5x7 to be shipped later, one to Utah, two to G.C... How does Ernest like things?

Uncertain that a letter would reach Emery before he left for Green River, Ellsworth wrote Blanche on 23 August 1911 and mailed the letter from the family home in Pittsburgh, Pennsylvania:

> ...I arrived home this A.M. after a very busy day in Rochester. I suppose Emery will still be home when this arrives so I will tell him what I did.
> I ordered a stereo hawkeye out of stock. They make them now to take 3½ x 3½ film and the exposed part is exactly stereo size. There is lots of edge to give ⅛ in more leway. They make the new model extra

wide bed and heavy posts on side of lens etc., very strong. Have ordered Zeiss Tessar lens' focus ⅜ inches shorter than the regular, auto duplex (8) shutter same as 3¼ x 4¼. ray screens to screw on to lens.

I ordered   50 -1 doz. rolls speed film   3½ x 3½

50 -1 doz. rolls   "   "   3¼ x 4¼

30 -10 ex   "   speed   3¼ x 5½

packed as for tropics also 4 cans slip top to contain all films.

The moving picture film order was transfeered from Broulatour to Eastman. Broulatour perforates some of his own film and I thought best to avoid that. The M.P. film is to be shipped with the other film c/o The Denver Photo Materials Co.

The films (small) and the stereo are billed through the Denver people... Did not get a binocular. Will write from here. I am sending a letter for Emery c/o Denver people with the trunk check and safe deposit check for the camera. I never got that screw for the M.P. Camera but have sent the address of a firm in Denver who will fix him out. They are City Novelty Works, 1027 19th St. Denver Colo. Dadman got some made. I did not get developing tanks as they are quite heavy. Dadman says not to get one for the hypo as the metal don't stand up but to have a flat box and put it in flat instead of on edge. He had just received a lot of work from Schneider and they were fierce. They were put into the box wet and stuck and dirty. They say his machinery is fine but work rotten.

Advise Emery.

1. We have advised baggage people not to send trunk to unclaimed baggage. He will have excess to pay.
2. To get camera out and get extra screws.
3. Boats were shipped with only 150 ft rope should have least 100 ft. beside 25 ft. on each for tying. Get 100 ft. there.
4. Get sockets and iron standards to go around cockpit for canvass.
5. I did not get canvass. Better get it there.
6. I shipped 1 case 8x10 speed plates to Denver. Take 3 doz. out for Green River, Wyo. Ship balance to Green River, Utah. Take chemicals also. Everything but bromide is with plates.

Ellsworth and Emery's younger brother, Ernest, came from Pittsburgh

to work at the studio for the duration of the river trip. As a reminder
Emery prepared a list of duties before leaving the Canyon:

> Work given to Earnest Aug. 1911 by E.C.K.
> First of all sales room to be cleaned & pictures straightened always
>   before 8 am. Plates loaded and developer made in evening.
> Work room straightened in eve. Lamps filled & cleaned.
> Snow always scraped off up to B.A. as soon as falling snow stopped.
> E.V. to tend to making his own bed and tend to room daily.
> Keep wood chopped if nothing else to do.
> Not to permit visitors during working hours and smoking in work
>   room etc. forbidden.
> Trays to be cleaned daily.
> Never to depend on us; to do work at any thing seen to be done.

The Racine Boat Works notified Emery of the shipment of the boats on
24 August:

> We are in receipt of your favor of 19th inst., and beg to advise the two
> boats have gone forward to Green River, Wyoming, and a draft was
> sent with the B/L. In the mean time however, your brother sent us a
> check from New York which entirely balanced your account with us;
> we have therefore instructed our bank here to re-call the draft and
> B/L from Green River, and we will enclose it either to you at Green
> River, or Grand Canyon which ever place you instruct. Please do not
> fail to instruct us where to send this B/L...
>   Enclosed we hand you a shipping receipt covering the middle
> section, oars, and strips which we have sent forward to Grand
> Canyon...

Emery had further correspondence with Evans on August 24:

> Yours of the 22nd, is at hand.
>   Glad we can reach you on short notice as I have not as yet heard
> from my brother as to the date we will meet at Green River.
>   As to the salary we propose to pay as follows. Your wages start

from the date you leave San Francisco. We pay your ticket transportation to Green River not including meals or berth.

We are to supply all grub for the trip and pay you on leaving the party $40. per month from the date you leave your town.

If finishing the trip with us to Needles we then will pay your ticket transportation back to San Francisco.

I may join you in your city but in case my brother wants me to meet him in Denver I will forward transportation on to you.

Hoping this is satisfactory to you and that our trip will be as good as we are contemplating,...

Emery left Grand Canyon in the evening of 28 August on the Santa Fe's Grand Canyon railroad for the first leg of the trip to Green River, Wyoming, and wrote a note to Blanche en route on 29 August:

Just got up and am nearing Winslow so will see if I can get this on todays train. I had a good sleep in Williams and hope you did not lay awake.

It is mighty cool along here and the grass along just looks dandy. Be good and don't worry or just be as good as you can.

Again he wrote to his wife from La Junta, Colorado, on 30 August:

Dear Blanche.

Here I am allready to take my train to Denver. There is a west train waiting for me to write this so I'll not say much. T'was mighty cool this morning and feels like frost. Just sent Edd a gram. I would be there at 2 P.M. today. Spent 80 ¢ yesterday for meals. How's that. I dread the 6 hours ride from here to Denver.

Love from your garlic top

Emery

Evans previously had applied for employment with the Post Office and was called to work making it impossible for him to carry out his plans to act as a third man on the trip. Emery's letter to Blanche 31 August indicates Evans had found a replacement he felt suitable for the trip:

My dear Wife,

Rec'd a wire from Edd on the train yesterday to stop off at Colo. Springs a day or two as some shipments are delayed, but we were past there when I got it. Edd looks ok but a couple of days may do us both good. Just rec'd a message from Evans who has a third man for us... You had better write me to Green River in answer to this I guess. I'll have time to get it and tell me how you are getting along. I am certainly pleased with the stereo Edd got, it is a peach. It seems that nothing is here everything delayed except what Edd brought ...

At Denver last minute details were attended to and Emery wrote Blanche on 31 August:

Today we accomplished quite a lot, and the world looks brighter. We received today all our films right from Eastmans. We recd a card from Maggie that papa had just shipped our beds to Green River and that they received word from the rest of the people that everything was shipped. We have been shopping all day and are about finished.

Got my red underware, gum soled shoes, 2 flannel shirts duck back pants & coat and what groceries etc. we wanted here. We will likely leave tomorrow evening for Green River.

We have a swell room with bath & 2 beds at $3.50 per day. Ed has gone out tonight to a show with Hattie West who we ran accross waiting table in the hotel we are staying. It seemed good to see her...

The Denver people are very nice and we just using there place as a storeall until we pack... We have certainly got a mess of stuff to take from here.

We are taking a developing tank so nearly everything in small films on the first part of our trip will be developed as we go...

With love to both my little girls.

And again on 1 September:

Well this will be my last letter from Denver. We have got everything now except a shutter which can follow. We are going to take a man with us that Evans recomended. He will be at Green River Sunday evening so we will likely leave there on Tuesday if boats and things are O.K... Myers did not mark excess on trunk so we got it here for nothing. That is worth something as there is 72 lbs. excess...

... We have arranged with a vault to hold our stuff we send them after reaching Green River Utah...

The last segment of the trip to Green River, Wyoming, began 2 September and Emery wrote a note to his wife en route:

We are now nearing G. River. Are on a very good fast train. The country we passed through is very uninteresting being sand doons and dryier than Ariz. The earlier part of the morning was long stretches of plains and good cattle country.

While I think of it have Earnest put a nail above the windows upstairs, his and Edd's room. That upstairs window is too near the trail since I fixed the side to be left open. I haven't had a word from you since I left. Hope there is something here. Evans' man will be here tomorrow night... We are shipping by frt. from Denver our grips which will go with the plates etc...

How is E.V. getting along with the work, and are my two little girls being as good as papa would have them.

I'll have to wash up now as we are near our destination and will write later.

With love from your husband, I am

Sincerely
Emery

A series of letters written from Green River, Wyoming tell their own story:

Sept 2nd 1911
Green River Wyoming.

Dear Blanche.-

I mailed you a letter just as we arrived but now since we have looked around I can tell you how things look.

I was surprised you had not written to me since I left, still you want me to write twice a day.

The boats are here in good order and are certainly fine. As yet they have not sent the bill of laden so we can't take them out until receiving this.

We will not get started until Tuesday or Wednesday. Everything is here now except the boxes which will go to Utah.

We went over to the river which is pretty & clear and as wide as the foot of the trail.

It is about 5 ft. deep.

We are staying at the UP. Hotel but is second class.

Ellsworth just got some postals of the town so I will send you one. Now you can write us to Jensen Utah which is on the river 12 mi. from the ~~the river~~ Vernal. Then any mail you want us to look over to answer or anything write us to Green river Utah and on all mark Hold until called for.

We will be there in about 20 days we think although Stone took 28 days for that distance When we get that far we will likely wire you.

The weather is cloudy and cool looks like storm.

When we got down to the river and saw fish we felt like when we were kids, and wanted our boats right away. They are certainly fine and much better than Stones. They are certainly decked right and could hold as much luggage again as we are taking.

The river is extremely low and people say is too low for boating. We see the remains of a steam boat on the shore and the store keeper has a motor boat. I would like to have an engine in ours for a while although going down stream we will not nead one.

The country is much like Winslow, except there is an island with trees and the pretty green water.

With love to you all and hoping you are going to write to me I am your loving husband

    Emery

I will write you several times before ~~this~~ we leave but in answer write us to Jensen Via. Vernal Utah.

    Good by

Sept 3, 1911

Dear Blanche.-

This seems a long day and tomorrow will be the same as Monday is the labor day and everything closed same as today.

Edd & I took a walk up the river on the R.R. tracks and it is certainly pretty. The water is as green and clear as glass and is not bad to drink. Why don't you write a line and let me know how you are...

This is a R.R. town and much like Winslow. Everyone thinks we will have it hard on account of the low water but we would rather get out and push occaisonally than to have high water in rapids.

We will have 100 mile smoothe water. Be sure and write to Jensen via. Vernal Utah. in answer to this letter and after that to Green River Wyoming [*Utah*].

Hope everything is going well and that you love your honey bunch enough to at least write a post card.

    With Love

    Emery

Sept. 4 1911

Dear Blanche.-

I am just in receipt this morning of your letter in answer to mine from Lamy.

We are in receipt of a letter from Denver saying your plates were shipped. They are also shipping our grips by freight. They have shipped us to here everything coming.

The only thing now is we can't get our boats out until the Bill of Lading comes. We may have to wire for it.

It is certainly fine we have these few days to rest up in, it is showing on us both. Ed is getting fat and over his nervousness all ready. I feel the better for the rest myself. This is a dandy cool fine air. Received a nice letter from Dave Rust this morning... Recd a message from Ralph [Cameron][16] that he would be here on the 29th last month. Hope he is there before going back to Wash...

Glad all are well and if you saw the nice outfit and the prospects of a dandy outing you'd never worry...

Sep. 5th 1911

Dear Blanche.

Just sitting down in a Chink restaurant. Used pears soap this morning and washed in the Green River. Yesterday afternoon we took all but our boats set up our tent and started to straighten things out.

The tent is a pale green, does not hurt the eyes and can not be too highly recomended.

We put our dark room up and loaded our plates. Got our focal plane and other shutters on our cameras and everything is just dandy.

Our folding table and shelves are great, so is everything else, and if you were to see the downy blankets and our sleeping bags which we occupied last night, there's no use talking you'd be jealous. Everything is just swell and no millionair could be fixed nicer.

We are in hopes we receive word from Racine today so we can get out our boats.

We have plenty clothing etc. in fact I believe we will be sending some of our stuff back from Utah. Now if our moving picture camera works right everything will be lovely. Not a thing was broke in all our express or baggage.

The setting of our camp with the balmy air and the glimmer of the moon on the water beside our camp gave a picture and feeling I'll not forget, just wished you was here to enjoy it…

We have a dandy hand tool out fit and was simply great in fixing up our lenz flanges etc.

My hot cakes are on now so I will close. Will write you this afternoon again.

With love from
Emery

Later in the day Emery wrote again:

Yours & Earnests just here.
Dear Blanche-
I promised to write again this afternoon so I will start in. I went

over town this morning and ordered our groceries and things. Nothing more has developed yet on the boats but on account of yesterday being labor day they may not have got my message until today.

It is blowing to beat the band and feels like snow so I put on my red underware. They are not as heavy as I thought they were but heavy enough.

I am certainly fixed fine and warm in every way so no matter what the weather is like I cannot get wet or cold. I have woolen shirts & socks beside sleeping socks and those wrestling pants and two swetters. The hunting suit I got is supposed to be water proof, beside Edd got those thin rubber shirts that go down to my feet.

This tent is a dream and if it stands the wind we are having now it will go through anything. We have certainly got a camp outfit. The dark room would be most too heavy to pack over the desert. It is three ply heavy cloth, over six ft. high and is long enough for two to sleep in. We would not have neaded any other tent having it, if the out cover had been water proof...

Edd just got back from town and nothing doing yet. I can't think up a long letter in a month and don't see how you expect me to write two a day. Morris has a graphaphone like ours and it made me homesick for ours so I went to the store and bought a mouth organ and will have a band by myself... We are fixed nicely to develope films or plates just as easy as if home and with our new lenzes and shutters we should work wonders...

Ed is writing out titles for the books and is fine to be in from the wind & rain. Just as safe as if at home with a better bed to sleep on. Of course it isn't just the same you know as if you were in it, but there is just room for one any way.

My wool feel quite good now in this cold air. This just 66 ft lower than home and is about the same when a cold rain strikes it. Isn't it fine when you think that we have everything here perfect just as we want it. It is raining and blowing to beat the band but I would rather it would rain today than tomorrow for if everything goes right we will start tomorrow noon. We don't want to start if dull as we wish to make a moving picture of our start. I got some gloves this morning so not to spoil my lily white hands with the oars. I have at my right hand side the book of The Desert as well as Edd's feet with a marvelous effect of green socks.

We have a large alcohol stove and 1 gal. grain alcohol in qt. cans. also cigar lighters.

Well the wind and rain now ceasith and my stomach feels the nead of a beef stake.

I will write tomorrow and let you know how things are.

> Love to all
> Emery

Sep 6 11.

Dear Blanche.

I guess this will be the last few lines for a while. I will also wire you a night letter this eve. We have been held up on account of several things but all is ok. now.

Our man from Frisco will be in town in an hour and a half and then we will pull out of town right away unless something else comes up. Everything is lovely and we are certainly buisy bees getting things together.

I will write in about a week from Linwood as I think there is a P.O. there then from Jensen via-Vernal Utah and then Green River Utah. so you see it won't be so bad after all.

We set up our darkroom this morning and snapped some pictures and developed them as well as motion, just to get our times right.

We moved our stuff accross the river so there wouldn't be so many bums hanging around. We have an awful lot of work yet in fixing up places for extra oars etc. and may just get out of town for a little way so we wont be bothered and then make our real start tomorrow.

Now dear don't you worry about me one bit cause all our stuff is just right and at this stage of water it will be next to impossible to have any misshaps and even so it could only be a delay on our boats. It has been mighty cold and I got a little of it but is fine and warm now.

The water is clear and beautiful as I sit on my folding camp stool and gaze upon it occasionally. Tell Earnest to do the best he can and help you.

He had better have the freight hauled. Now dear I give you one good kiss also edith and you be good girls until I show up and then be better.

Good by sweetheart
Lovingly
Emery.

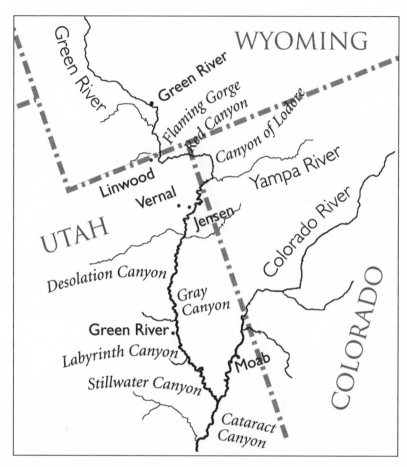

on transcription formatting

THE AUTHOR of each passage is indicated by his first name in the margin. To help set them apart, each author has a distinctive typeface.

Emery   Emery C. Kolb

Ellsworth   **Ellsworth. L. Kolb ("Ed" or "Edd")**

Bert   **Hubert R. Lauzon ("Bert")**

September 6   The date appears in the margin as do occasional contemporary place names to orient the reader.

part two
Green River, Wyoming
to
Green River, Utah

Green River

Got release on our boats and hauled them to camp. Emery rowed up to turn. Camp on West side. Cold.

J. Fagen came 3:10. Shopped until evening. Baggage on West shore. Took everything on boat to bridge.

After several days of anxiety we waited for the arrival of our third man, James Fagan, who finally came Sep. 7th.

Taking a moving picture of our boats and a small party and a small party who came to see us start, we pulled out of Green River at 9:30 am, Friday the 8th. Water was clear and low and on several occasions we got on shoals with the boats which compelled us to get out and push.

Everything went lovely until the first stretch of swift water was approached. This was a division of the river and proved to be the smaller amount of the river. The force of the water was directly again the bank which held a sharp curv. Here a large green cottonwood was laying in the watter in which Edd's boat was cast. At first looked as though the cockpit would be filled but came out safely. Twelve miles down we came upon a ranch where we met two fine young fellows named Logan and asked us have dinner. We are spending the night here and developing a plate to test a camera.

September 8
Ellsworth · C[amp] 1

Groceries loaded. 9:30 A.M. started moving picture of start and showing Bridge. 2 miles down Emery shot duck. Farther down saw several. One little riffle Grounded twice and ran into a tree fallen down. 3 P.M. came to Logan ranch two boys. Camped. Took views

news item · *The* Coconino Sun *ran an article on Sunday, 8 September* 1911:

HAVE COMMENCED PERILOUS TRIP
Kolb Brothers Started on Long Dangerous Journey Through Grand Canyon by Boat

The following letter was received this week from Kolb brothers, the two daring young photographers on the eve of their departure down the Green River into the Colorado river and through the Grand Canyon by boat. Since Major Powell first made this trip years ago, in boats built by the government especially for the trip, no white men have attempted the passage. Many persons have been down the Colorado river, the most treacherous stream in the west, and their bodies never recovered:

Green River, Wyoming,
Sept. 2, 1911.

Mr. F.S. Breen, Flagstaff, Arizona
Dear Mr. Breen:

Some weeks ago you gave notice in your paper of our contemplated trip for still and motion pictures through the Green and Colorado rivers, so we thought you may be interested in knowing the time of our departure is at hand.

We have everything gathered together including our boats and moving picture camerias and all looks satisfactory. We expect to leave Wednesday Sept. 6th, and if we get through the 1400 miles successfully we will arrive at

The Brave Ones

KOLB BROS PASSING RIVERTON UT
GREEN RIVER WYOMING TO
BRIGHT ANGEL ARIZONA.

Needles before the new year. The town people here look on us as a physician might a hopeless case and then relate weird stories of others who attempted the voyage and never heard from again.

The town of Green River may be compared with Winslow, being a railroad town with bleak sand domes in the distance.

The beautiful water of Green River aids to attract the place but we are glad to be on our way back to the towering walls and the aroma of the pine in northern Arizona.

    Yours Truly
    Kolb Bros.

            Logans Ranch Sept 9th 1911   letter from
Dear Blanche-   Emery

  I suppose you will be surprised to hear we are only 10 or 12 miles down the river. We had so much to fix with our oar locks and places to carry extra ones that we stopped here yesterday afternoon finding two agreeable fine fellows here who offered us their black smith shop and everything else which would have taken us 3 or four days anywhere on our trip and then not so satisfactory.

So we will stay here tonight and tomorrow Sunday just move on a little so not to impose on good nature.

Now have Earnest do up a three dollar book and a cloud and duplicate and mail to Dave Logan Green River Wyoming. We had a nice little run down here and feel great confidence in our out fit. Our Frisco man is Jimmie Fagan and is certainly the man. He is a kid 22 years husky, neither drinks nor uses tobacco and the greatest trouble he wants to do everything himself. He is certainly ok and says he will stick as long as we do.

I got a duck shortly after we left town and roasted it here last night. We see fish by the thousands some very large. The river is so clear one can see 10 ft. down.

The river is very low and we have to get out and push the boat off the shoals.

It will be quite slow work for some time on account of the low water. We will get new supplies at Linwood there is a post office there and is in Utah but you will not have time to write there Jensen is the place for you to write via Vernal, and be sure to send us some money to get supplies and take our freight out for we just have five dollars.

This is one of the prettiest places you can imagine.

The log cabin is located under a grove of large cottonwoods and is flat, then the river passing within 50 ft of the house. We paid $6 for our shotgun and I got a duck the first shot.

Well dear I guess this is all this time and I will write to you as soon as we get to Linwood Utah. Love to you all. Your own hubby.

Emery

letter from
Emery

Dear Blanche-

This is the name of a ranch man who has been very kind to us. Kindly do up one of our $3.00 hand colored books and mail to the address above as soon as possible. We did not know we could mail this and just have to hurry. We are getting along fine but on acct of low water could not make any faster time.

Our next stop will be at Lodore P.O. but you can't write to there— write to Jensen and be sure to have money there as we are broke.

With love to all
From your loving

Husband
Emery

September 9
Emery

Worked on boat at ranch nearly all day. Made a ... [*illegible*] mile run down to Fire Hole peaks and find a beautiful camp stayed there for Sunday.

On the way down saw many herron. Edd shot coyote but did not get him.

One hour after setting line caught 14 lb. salmon.

Worked on boats all day. Fixed oar locks and extra oars.

Ellsworth

September 10
Emery

Put up our tent and stretched out on our beds. Jimmie entertains us with songs.

C 2 Made a little run to Fire Hole Chimneys. Grounded twice. Rested all day in camp. Very warm. Evening. Snagged a little bull head set line caught a 14 lb. white fish. Beaver sign.

Ellsworth

September 11
Emery

Left our camp and pulled down stream most all day as there was little current was slow except where shoals hastened it along but on their account we climbed out of our boats to get it off the sandbars. The water was beautifull and clear and in the river we saw thousands of fish. Nooned at Black Fk. and ammused ourselves watching black eagles soar above us. About six in the evening Ellsworth discovered a man, Mr. Holmes plowing. Being informed we might obtain some eggs from them we stopped our boats and found some fine people. Two visiting ladies and our cook James entertained with song.

Warm Clear

Ellsworth

Made a good run with few stops. Shot a small duck and spent some time hunting. Low rolling hills. Noon Black's Fork. Deep pools lots of fish in sight thin shoals. 5 P.M. Struck Walter Holmes Ranch P.O. Box #[*number omitted*]

Firehole Chimneys

Camped on river at Ranch spent a plesant evening at the ranch. Music. C.3.

September 12

Emery Leaving Holmes ranch we drifted down some of the finest scenes in my life. Cottonwoods, maples vining Clemitus and other bushes frost colored. Passed Ridger bottom where 8 year old boy stood out with rifle to protect his home. Saw his father afterwards at Linwood. Passed another ranch and nooned on a beautiful plot under cottonwoods. Covered up on acct of shower. Camped at night on island. Had heavy fog in morning.

Ellsworth **Warm. River about the same. grounded a few times Lots of eagles. Each one got a duck. Lots more in sight. Passed Bridger Bottom Ranch at noon. Little riffles Made a long run. Camped on an Island. C.4**

September 13

Emery Made a good run down to Henry Fork. encountered rain and wind blowing up stream made waives like ocean. nooned at 2 P.M. ate a bite and left Jimmie with boats while EL and I walked to Linwood. Wrote

Henrys to wife and after purchasing provisions started back. Heavy rain, dark,
Fork and lost our bearings until hearing Jim snoar we found our camp.

Ellsworth **Morning cold and cloudy. Mist on the river and frost. Reached Henry's**

Fork at noon. Wind very strong upstream still water and hard rowing water getting muddy. Emery and I walked to Linwood in the P.M. very hard rains. Pretty villiage. Got some interesting information from the men at the store.

~~Got~~ Took supper at the hotel walked back after dark. Got lost near river. Heard Jim snore. C 5.

Linwwood Utah

Sept 13 1911
Linwood [4]

letter from Emery

Dear Blanche.

Here we are down to Linwood and I have walked five mile to drop this letter. The store keeper just said 6 mile. Well we have had a fine trip. All the way down are just the places that my heart allways pine for. We have all the fish and ducks we want and could have more if we needed it. We are now in Utah and while I stand at the window of the P.O. writing you it is just pouring down rain. This little country village is right in the Uinta mountains and is surely beautifull along the Henry Fork creek. We just got about 20 lb. of provisions to last till we get to Jensen Utah where you are to send us ten dollars or so and be sure to have $100.00 or so at Green River Utah. We will We will be to Jensen in 10 to 15 days for certain. Our helper is an Irish good natured kid. On two occasions we have been the guests of ranchers. The last one we struck was a man and wife with two girls visiting. There we found a piano and one of the girls was a dandy player. Jimmie is a fine singer and we just had a dandy time enjoying it with fresh buttermilk. It is anything so far but what we expected as we have struck nice ranches all the way. Be sure to write me a nice letter to Jensen and another to Green River.

I hope E.V. is doing nicely and that my little girl is just as good as you are. It is time for the P.O. to close now so once more I will send all my love to you and baby.

Good by dear
Emery

Cloudy. Started 9.20 Moving picture of entrance to our 1st canyon Flaming Gorge.

September 14 Emery

Flaming Gorge

Ran two small rapids. Saw 2 beaver and geese. Nooned opposite old ranch with crude dock or old ferry.

Scenes beautiful. Rock fell in middle of river near my boat. Camped at Sheep Creek.

Ellsworth **Cloudy. C 6**

Start 9.20. Took a short moving picture of the entrance to Flaming Gorge. Color of red rocks like algonquin. Ran two little rapids without trouble Saw 2 beaver and some geese. Camped noon opposite ranch. Reached Sheep Creek or Kingfisher (Powell) 4 P.M. Beautiful scene. Three peaks on right like "Three Brothers[5]" Overhauled our boats. Camped at Creek.

September 15

Emery Very Hot.

Started 10 A.M. after going up Sheep Creek where I caught two beautifull trout.

Shoals where we grounded several times and many long quiet stretches wher we rowed hard in quiet water. Ran several small rapids, then came to one much larger at an old boat landing or ferry where Ed struck a couple of rocks we nooned between two rapids and took off our skags as rapid was very rocky.

Then lined our first rapid where Powell upset in. River descended rapidly. Passed Kettle Creek about 5 P.M. Ran about 4 more rapids one we thought bad proved nice water.

Made another safely with Jim in my boat but both struck rocks and just missed one bad one. Camped by a small stream where some one else had camped within a year or two.

Ellsworth **Hot**

Start at 10. First went up stream a short distance. Emery caught 2 trout. Long quiet stretches and shoals where we grounded two or three times and several very small rapids then a big one near an old boat landing. Went below and looked it over. Ran it safely but touched one or two rocks, Jim staying below with a life preserver and rope. Another long shallow rapid which we ran then a third where we saw some geese but they got away. Looked it over and decided we could run

the upper half. Did it easily. Swift current and lots of rocks. Landed below on island. Crossed to ~~left~~ (r) bank. Noon. Took off our skags. Lower end too shallow and rocky. Beautiful view Rocks reddish brown 1500 ft. high. Lined boats down, safely, made a moving picture (Same rapid Powell party upset in.[)] Steep slope to whole river and sharp turns. Ran about four rapids one had a long easy shoot which we had looked over and made safely then a quick turn to the right with Emery leading, Jim in his boat. Wave lifted each of us over a hidden rock. Ran on again and I got on wrong side of River and could not land and went over largest rapid encountered. Touched a rock or two at the start and made the shoot safely. Emery landed above and sent Jim below and did the same. Camped at a small stream on South side. Signs of old camp. C 7

(Passed Kettle Creek about 5 P.M.)

Clear.

Left camp 8.20 after fishing a little. Ran 3 rapids then came to a bad one. Sent Jim below with rope and life preservers while I ran the rapid. Edd took moving pictures. ~~los~~ dropped extra oar & pole. Ed lost his pole. ...of my run. Struck two rocks and on one ran up on it. ~~lined Ed's boat, lined Ed's boat~~ Ran another and both struck rocks. I ran another then lined Ed's boat as rocks bad. Noon on S.S. after lunch ran out on

September 16
Emery

Removing skeg

shallow stretch and landed above bad rapid. Edd starts out and gets in a nest of rocks he lands also above rapid. Sent Jim below where water makes quick turn to bank of rocks and mistakes the place goes below whole rapid.

I run the rapid but was unable to keep out, and seeing I was going to get in wrong let my boat run up on rock near bank where Jim was told to be ready.

Got in all right alone and did not hurt the boat.

Was afraid E would do the same but he wanted a picture running the rapid so I stationed Jim below to catch him or stop a direct blow again the short turn. Jim turned him as he was striking and E made the rapid safely. Ran several more one being a very long one and full of rocks. Stopped to camp. But on acct. of cactus ran another rapid and camped opposite a little stream coming in on the South.

Here we camped for Sunday and were all ready for it as we had a hard day and by the maps just made a few miles. Ran about 15 rapids but were not yet to Ashley falls. Jim fell twice bruised a toe and we are all glad a 7th day had been set apart. Ed puts his boat on dry dock as it is leaking.

Ellsworth **Clear. AM. Cold. Day hot.**

Start about 9 A.M. ran two small rapids then lined both boats down a rocky one. Ran a bunch of small rocky ones and three bad ones. Emery took a picture of me as I was coming down a bad one and my oar lock pulled out. Had a hot time for a little while and hit several rocks, one of them hard. Emery ran a bad one and concluded I had better line my boat. Took a moving picture of E.C. running the rapid. Noon on the south side, just a lunch then at it again. Canyon is very impressive and the River has a decided drop even where there are no rapids. We proceed cautiously and don't make much time. Keep looking for Ashley Falls but do not reach it. Camp at a nice open spot on the north side at a side canyon with another on the south side with a small stream. All of us very weary, glad tomorrow is Sunday. C 8

September 17

Emery Clear & Cool.

Stayed in bed until late then E & I walked down to see if the rapid we heard was Ashley Falls. I got a cotton tail with my 6 shooter. We climbed the mountain about 1400 ft. and get splendid view. See ranch on S. S. and Jim and E go out in afternoon. Return at 5 P.M. Woman & 4 children in recent homestead. one days ride to Vernal or Linwood.

Red Canyon Sept 17 1911

Dear Blanche,-

This is Sunday and I am sure glad for I was tirid. The water is so low that it takes more work and more time too, to get through and we may be a few days longer getting to Jensen than we expected.

Ed & I climbed a hill this morning and saw a ranch so decided to go to it and see if we could drop this note with them.

Everything has been going fine but good hard work.

Got a rabbit this morn and will stew it with rice for the boys when they get back.

If we don't get through just as quick as we expected don't get alarmed as the low stage of water makes it more work.

We had some fine trout yesterday plenty duck and today rabbit. We see many deer track but have not seen any as yet. I hope you and E.V. are getting along OK with the work. I think of you all the time and hope you are not worring. We wear our preservers all the time even though we don't think it necessary. A kiss for you both. Lovingly

Emery

Emery and I climbed up an old deer trail on the north side and got a wonderful view of the mountains and the winding River. Wonderful coloring. Dark green of the pines and firs on the high mts. Yellow and red mixed in the quaking aspen gray spots in the parks "brown stone fronts" in the walls very light green in the willows leafed cottonwood at the rivers edge and in side canyons and mountains everywhere. The canyon is very crooked and turns everywhere. Had our binoculars along and discover a ranch on the south side high up (1300 ft.). Come back to camp and each write a letter to B & home. Jim and I climb to the ranch taking two hours. Find a woman and four children at work in the garden. Woman rather frightened ask her to see that the letters

Ellsworth

are mailed and she gladly promises. Four other ranches near. Take a deer trail back to camp one hour. Night cold.

September 18

Emery Clear but cloudy windy night. Calked E's boat up with gum etc. Ran 17 rapids counting Ashleys Falls. one rapid about ¾ miles long with great descent filled with rocks, and boats hit many but having under controle did not damage much.

Ashley
Falls E ran Ashley Falls hits stern on large rocks lost extra oars. I follow and tip rocks but made quite clear run. Jim took moving picture. camped just below the fall.

Ellsworth C 9

Make a fine start and run one rapid after another until we have put 11 behind us at noon last one had a million rocks and we couldn't miss them all Got a couple hard bumps. River still has rapid fall. I am learning some and get through fairly well.

Mon. 18. P.M.

I get Jim in my boat and we run 5 rapids in quick succession one of them bad.

The river is not rough but slides along like oil but has a tremendous force behind it. A rock jumps up in front of you an inch or two below the surface. Your boat does not appear to move but the rock is coming for you like a shot you watch it fascinated as you are drifting down stern first, the bow pointed a little one way or the other and you idly dip your paddles to keep the boat under control. Suddenly you realize you are on top of the rock the stern has passed but the bow will surely strike. You spring into action and give a mighty ~~mighty~~ strong pull on the off side oar and if you have time back water a little with the other then lift it quickly over the rock to strike in again as rocks are jumping up all around you and it is dodge here and swing there, and you involuntarily lean to one side when you find you are at last drifting broadside towards a high one. You strike and the boat shivers and swings around with the bow out.

If the current is strong you may drift off or you may have to push off with an oar or pole or even get out in the water and lift if it is not too deep and swift. Then a long smooth stretch and you give a sigh of

contentment and lean back on your oars or even in the long rapids after passing a swift rapid past a rock you will drop into a lee way below
the rock and rest undisturbed and find it is hard work sometimes to
get the boat into the current. 16 rapids up to 2.30 P.M. and at last you see
ahead the barrier you have been looking for for two days; Ashley Falls.
A dozen immense boulders have fallen from the right side stopping
the channel completely or at least so it seems from some points but
you find there is a crooked channel 12 ft. wide that a boat just can go
through. We take some moving pictures of the approach and leaving
one boat down with the rope so we can get the cameras in place etc.

Another party has run the shoot and we conclude to risk it. I am
ready first but have swung a little too much toward the right and cannot use the right oar and go through straight. As soon as possible I
pull on both oars but the full force of the River pent up in a 12 ft channel is forcing against the rock in the center and pull as you will your
boat is hurled against it striking a corner of the stern. You notice one
of your spare oars has fallen in the water and try to pick it up when the
bow swings around and strikes also and the other oar goes over but
you let them go and pull to safety which fortunately lies close below.
You pick up your oars at leisure then look back and see your brother
coming through cool and collected and he just touches the rock and
swings around bow first and comes out smiling. We find Ashleys
name faintly written under a rock. We camp on the sand 100 yds below
the rock. Ashley F. C 10.

Clear

Stayed at Ashley falls from 2.30-18 until 12.15 P.M. 19

pictured remains of Ashley's name just above Powells trail where
stones were placed to carry boats around.

Painted our autographs on rocks where Gal. & Stone chiseled theirs.

Named & painted my boat for my daughter Edith. Left camp 12.15
and immediately plunged into water filled with rocks.

Our 4th rapid though smaller was much the appearance of Ashley
with rocks out in the river.

Alltogether ran 19 rapids. The last 4 or 5 being decided drop to the
river. One with ledge shooting* clear accross. Struck and got hung up

on several rocks but not to damage the boat. Finding a very bad one coming, landed Jim on shore. Hung up on rock in bad water. Ed passed, landed and I did not move my boat from rocks until pictures were made of my perdicament.

After running this we ran one long rapid ½ mile and camped about 1 mile above Ashley Park or Little Browns Hole. Made moving pictures through the afternoon.

*shipped water

Ellsworth **(19 rapids)**

Spend the morning at Ashley's Falls. Start at 12.15 P.M. Run 3 little rapids then a big one some what like Ashleys a number more small ones then the canyon gets very deep and impressive and the rapids are very long and rocky. In one we take a moving picture of Emery coming down and a short film of myself but it gets chopped up. I run one rapid a[nd] bump a number of times but get through safely. Emery follows and gets hung up on a rock the bow sticking in the air. He assures us he is O.K. and I take a number of pictures of him. Camp near a dry side canyon on the north side among the pines. C 11.

September 20

Emery Clear

Having trouble with moving picture camera we did not leave until 12.15 P.M. ate lunch in Ashley Pk. ran several bad rapids. One which had bad fall decided to line then ran. E. first struck rock on acct. wind. I ran got hung on rock but went through safely.

Farther down river divides. Channel pushes directly again boulder in sharp curv. We both get in water and lower boats in smaller chanell. Get out of Red Canyon into Big Brown Hole. Get stuck on shoals.

Brown's Park

Tinted mountains in distance beautifull. Great color harmony.

Land at deserted ranch late and camp in front of ranch. Find later rancher had been killed. Shot in back & placed in his boat which was then pushed into river. Body found about 15 miles below. Evidently a learned man as his books were on astronomy and the like. pictures of his wife and all were hanging and every thing was deserted as it stood.[6]

C ɪɪ 12.

Have quite a time getting the M.P. Camera to work. Everything goes wrong. Get started at 12.15. Run 14 rapids before we lunch. Get out into Ashley Park or Little Browns Hole. Run 12 more rapids before evening. Get back into the Red Canyon again after A. Park as it is only a couple miles long. Great view of the mountains with autumn coloring.

Last of Canyon not so high but some very bad rapids. I get some *hard knocks. We line one very rocky rapid. Camp in Browns Park two mile below canyon. I get stuck on last rapid, a nasty little one with three ledges clear across and get some ugly knocks that don't do my boat any good. Camp at a deserted Ranch. All furniture in place and doors open.

*Wind very bad in 3 rapids and cause trouble in 2 rapids.

Clear

Left ranch at 9 am. travel through beautifull groves of cottonwood. river like Mosouri except more clear. see many geese & ducks. ~~Camp on the beautiful park. Find rancher in field with wife and children raking hay.~~ ["O.K. camp in spits [?] place" *written above (most likely referring to Spitz Bottom)*] Provisions from sheep man at Bridgport.

Ice in A.M. Clear & cold.

We run several small rapids counting 14 for the day. Strike a bad one in little canyon with barriers clear across about ¼ mile long but manage to make it with a few bumps I find I have split one bottom rib and a side plank a little. My boat leaks about 1 inch in the center. Jim gets in E.C.'s boat and rows while Emery steers. Go through Swallow Canyon that way. No rapids but a very hard pull against the wind. Come to a ferry in open where they are crossing sheep 2400, ½ doz. men. Foreman agrees to sell us some supplies. Helps a lot. In the P.M. we strap the two boats one ahead of the other and Jim and I row Emery steering. Still water with lots of shoals and we have to wade. Mts. in the distance lots of deserted ranches. Come to a beautiful grove of poplars with ranchmen harvesting hay near by. Camp 6 miles from Lodore P.O. Spitz [?] C 13. ~~dead mans~~

letter from
Emery

Ladore Colo.

Dear Blanche-   Sept 21 1911

I sent a little note today with a rancher but guess we will get to Ladore P.O. tomorrow before he gets it off. It is 9.30 and I am as tired as I care to be. Just finished sewing a gum sole on my shoes.

We are camped on as pretty a park as you can imagine. Saw some ranchers making hay so went over. It is as flat a piece of ground as I ever saw at the base of the mountain. There were about 5 men 4 children and the mother driving a rake to a fare you well. We got provisions from the rancher I want you to send the book to. They had a little girl and it makes me want to know how my little girls are getting along without dad. We have got about 45 cts. left so you see we will be glad to get a little at Jensen. We may not be there for a couple weeks. Made a long run today and got on quite a number sand bars. Well dear your old man is very tired and must close now. I hope everything is going well and that I will hear no bad news from you when you write with lots of love.

Emery.

September 22

Emery   Clear

Leave camp 9.

Pull down stream. bad up stream wind. tie boats together Jim & E row. I steer.

Afternoon row alone, run into snag and crack plank in *Edith*.

Great parks with deserted ranches under the cottonwoods.

Get information from Post Mistress whose two sons had ran Ladore Canyon. Mail letters at Ladore P.O. Girl or woman scared. Take picture of her three children in boat. Move on and camp at the head of Ladore.

Ellsworth   **Camp 14 mouth of Lodore.**

Steady pull all day long through a beautiful valley a few showers,

Gates of
Lodore   **take a few pictures of the cottonwood groves etc. Chat with the Lodore P.M. at a hay ranch. Reach the P.O. and mail a letter and some cards. Camp at mouth of Lodore. Most wonderful cut of its kind on earth. the River cuts into the mountain.**

Canyon of Lodore

Cloudy

Broak camp 9.30 ran 4 rapids and came on Winnies Grotto huge boulder in center of river. I lined my boat. Ed ran, oar slipped and stern hit boulder. no damage.

Ran 15 rapids more The last one disaster. ~~got stuck in~~

Ed ran upper part clear I struck side on rock. Started into lower end of Disaster, got stuck in head of it, fortunately. Carried provisions and all on island camped and next day being sunday, decided to make several days there. got supper in dark and shower adds to our discomfort.

Tired & wet.

Camp 15 at Island below upper Disaster Falls. We run four small rapids than come to a bad one. Large boulders and a narrow channel. Emery's ~~goes first~~ boat is lined down (4 lines for both boats) but he is feeling badly and we concluded to run mine. I strike the big center rock with one corner then swing through. Run five rapids in the P.M. some of them bad ones. Last one is U. Disaster Falls. Emery goes first and strikes the big boulder slightly but does no harm. I miss the left hand channel and take the right. Just squeeze through. Oars stick on rocks and shoot up past me. Emery wants to run the next rapid as the camp is bad. We start without looking rapid over and hang up on rocks. Pull boats high and dry and make a late camp.

Stringing wire to send luggage ashore

September 24

Emery Cloudy

Lined a wire across small part of river from island to shore below. (autograph on rock.) Ran all our luggage by pulley to shore. Lined boats down to new camp While taking moving picture of the let down I had to stop to assist Ed. as the current had caught his boat and was taking it down. Suceeded in second attempt after he caught rock by fingers. He came out but bruised. Camped here Sunday night. River had been fairly clear but recent rains muddied it although but very little rise

Ellsworth **Not a day of rest. ~~We line the boats down over the rapid~~ We string a wire across the short side of the island and run what we need to make a camp across. Put up tent etc. Rain in P.M.**

September 25

Emery Everyone although dead tired crawled out their blankets to gather luggage in tent. on acct. of let down everything was out. Rained quite hard and made camp miserable.

Damaged films & plates we had made for testing purposes. Ran luggage and transfered boats below (pictures) being busy and tired nights had to let notes go so have got incidents mixed. The let down where boat got him off his feet was today 24th.

Camped here Monday night and find we are between two bad rapids, Upper & lower Disaster. Lower runs [*continued under September 26*]

Line our boats down to camp on left side of rapid. Very rough water 50   Ellsworth
ft fall in Up. & lower Dis Rapid. Make M.P. of sending stuff across on
line also lining boats. I get beyond [illegible] lining boat and go 50 ft
down rapid holding to boat get out with Emery's help. In the evening
develope some films and plates. Rain.

September 26

with whole body of water to right wall which it has undermined and   Emery
would be certain death to try and run it. This being the worst and only
rapid we thought could not be run without destruction although we
did line some above.

The force of water runs under a shelving rock. Wi[d]th of whole river
from bank to cliff 21 ft. wide. We decide to take all luggage out carry it
below rapid and line boats empty. Eat lunch in boats out in river stuck
on rocks and then with full stomach we decide to try a let down with
full boats. We succeded successfully after about 2 hours hard wading
falling etc.

We then successfully ran 5 rapids and camp on beautifull spot on ~~left~~
right in deep canyon. ~~line one run.~~

Camp 16   Ellsworth
   Started late on acct rain, 11 A.M.
   Rowed a short distance then lined a rocky rapid rowed and landed
at head of Lower Disaster Rapid. Water goes under cliff 600 ft. straight
width at narrowest place 21 ft. Very bad rapid. Eat lunch then line it.
4 P.M. run 6 rapids by 5.30 one short one very high. Two rather bad.
Camp below side canyon on right near sugar loaf.

September 27

Hard rain and are now preparing in rain to leave. Time 11 am.   Emery
Looked over 1st. rapid and decide to run it see bad rock and start.
Current to great for me to controle so hang up on rock, boat turns
enough for water to pour in cockpit. Water runs in compartment
through bulkhead ruining 3¼ x 4¼ Kodak, grub and other valuables. E.
takes picture while boat hangs.

Boys throw rope and pull *Edith* to shore. Bail her and continue. Ran 2
more stiff ones and make a turn on one we consider dangerous. View superb so photograph it down stream to Dun's bute just below sugar loaf.

Force of water to left shore again large rock. *Edith* goes through successfully as well as a smaller one below. Jim stays below with rope in case of accident.

E. leads out an[d] in his strong effort to prevent being thrown again large rock on bank pulls to much to other side and strikes burried rock. Boat fills turns with Ed scrambling on top.

Jim runs to my boat for rope. I see oars seat etc. go down stream, run to boat and overtake them before being carried into

Jim looses my rope in water

Loose our guns next rapid. Boat gets in whirlpool and I have hard time rowing across to other side again. Out of Ed sight on account of bend in river. Jim calls Ed's boat is loose. I still ~~could not~~ had not controle of boat and see Jim wade out drawing in floating beds etc. the boat full of water strikes rock by Jim and he holds her.

For a moment I wonder what became of Ed. but a second thought I knew his life preserver would float him if he was off the rock. We throw him rope and pull him in. Find boat smashed on bottom and camp on sand. Everything was carried out and strewn on the sand to dry. Cameras moving picture films and all spoiled. We start to pitch tent but before it was completed a wind like a cyclone brought torrents of water from above.

Everything was blown on the wet sand. Destruction & misery.

When the heavy wind ceased the rain did not. We tied up our dark room and piled things pelmel into it.

Ellsworth **Cloudy C 17.**

We take a few pictures in the morning and re-arrange our boats. Get a late start 11 A.M. First rapid is rocky. Emery gets hung up on a rock and I pass him missing him by a short distance. Land below and take some pictures of him. Second rocky, I go first and mistake the channel but get through after bumping a few. Emery does better. Third looks bad large rock on left three big submerged rocks and big waves. Emery takes it and gets through and continues over a fourth. I start and am so anxious to miss the big rock that I land against a smaller one and before I know it my boat is on its side against the rock almost ⅔ under water and I climb over the side on top of the rock the

Ellsworth stranded

boat being held by the current. My oars float down stream and Emery runs for his boat to get them.

Meanwhile I get my bed and bags out of the boat on the rock. I am talking to Jim who is standing in the water near the shore when the boat suddenly breaks loose rights itself and goes down stream, the water released, rushes over the rocks and takes the bags after it. Jim runs down shore below the next rapid and rescues every thing Emery being caught in a stiff eddy and not being able to get to our side. He finally pulls through and attaches a life preserver to a rope and throws it to me after taking a couple pictures of me alone on the rock. I hold the rope and jump into the rapid and am surprised to find I can touch and wade to shore. The boat is ⅔ full of water and Emery has shipped a lot in the first rapid so nearly everything is soaked including cameras etc. and moving picture films, exposed. We have everything on shore drying and are just putting up the tent when a violent wind and rain starts and finishes the job completely.

I have lost the two guns in the impact. We get the tents up and eat a 4.30 P.M. lunch then go to work to find what is damaged are surprised to find all plates and films intact except the ex. moving picture film.

Work till late in the night. Then it rains some more for a change. C 17.

September 28
Emery

Next day was clear so we dried out with large ropes to hang clothes on.

Repair Ed's boat and work late into the night.

A recent storm had raised the river, the things were not wet with water but liquid mud. Make test & find 1/5 of river is mud. All this mud in sugar etc. gives a chocolate color.

Oatmeal wet so we cook whole box other things done likewise. The river rises 3 ft. E and Jim while at waters edge discover fish. Jim grabs one over 1 ft long. We neaded the grub. Getting into our boats we obtain 13 fish before breakfast by striking them with oars. Variety of suckers, bull head & bony tail. All work late and sleep in tent.

Jim's songs for the past week have ceased and at this camp he cries and talks of home & mother. He seems glad to know we will send him back to Frisco from Jensen

Ellsworth

Emery wakes me to tell me the river has raised 3 ft. and almost taken my boat away which was high and dry on shore.

We stretch our long rope back and forth and hang all clothes bags etc. out to dry building 3 fires Have a fine day and keep the same camp and get everything dry. I have a bad knock in the bottom of my boat and Emery puts in 5 hours repairing it and we put in some cotton and black paint. The fish. I almost forgot the fish story. Jim comes running to camp with a bony tail 15 in. long which he caught with his hands in the muddy water. We all go down and in 30 minutes we have 14 fish; one bull head 5 suckers and 8 bony tail, most of which we get by hitting with the oars sometimes cutting them almost in two. 11.30 P.M. and a cloudy sky Emery reports the biggest rapid yet just below us, the river has fallen almost to normal.

Camp 16. [written in error].

September 29

Emery

Drizzle

Repair on E's boat is fine. Leave Camp 11 am. carry luggage over bad rapid and line boats. Run 4 more rather stiff ones and come to very bad one at 4.10 PM. Carry luggage ¼ mile over boulders and line my boat.

Triplet
Falls

I get supper and we set tent up. Much drift wood. Build large fire and enjoy one of our finest camps. our ears seem to be getting immune to

Lining Triplet Falls

the roar of the water. Jim cries again tonight. Boys getting beds down and a rainy night is on.

Ellsworth   C 18

Leave camp at 11 again. Raining we cross to East shore and land at the head of a very big rapid but clear channell. We portage all baggage below set up the camera. ~~take~~ Emery takes a photo of me as I go through. Splash into the water and should make a showy picture. I make it safely, Emery follows, load up and on again. Run two more stiff ones then a quiet stretch and two small ones then another. Below this there is a long ~~quut~~ quiet stretch and back water so we look for a bad one below and are not dissapointed. We eat lunch first then go down and look it over. It is about ¼ mile long divided into three sections. The middle one running along the edge of the wall all are filled with bad boulders. This is possibly Triplet Falls. We portage all stuff from Emery's boat and line his boat. This takes 2½ hours. Then Jim and I carry the baggage from mine while Emery cooks supper. We have an ideal camp about 75 ft from the river against the rock wall. It is drizzling but we have put the tent up and have a big fire in front of the tent. There are big flat rocks all around to lay things on and Dunns Cliff as near as we can make out is right above us 2800 ft. high. This is the end of the Sierre Escalanta Mts. E & I both take a bath while Jim repairs his clothes. C 18.

September 30

Emery   Drizzle.

Leave camp 11.10.

Run one rapid and come to Hells half mile. Line my boat to head of rapid. Cottonwood tree 6 ft. diameter lodged again large rocks. Carry our luggage half mile to end of rapid. Climbing over trees boulders and 100 ft. on side of wall.

Hells
Half
Mile

Rain starts in while we work on boats, portaging them over rocks. Recent high water made slime covered rocks so slippery we fell dozens of times. We get *Edith* over worst rock & part of rapid just at dark.

We had prepared for rain and set up our tent so wet bruised & all scratched up we loaded our arms and dragged ourselves into camp for the night. Get my boat over.

C 19

We take a few pictures of our camp and canyon also one showing   Ellsworth
lining my boat in the last of Triplet Falls. Glad to get through it. Start
out at 11 and strike a long still pool and know from that we are coming
to Hells Half Mile. It's all of that and then some. Great boulders are
scattered all through the river and there is a fall of possibly 15 ft. in 50
with the current shooting in a doz. different directions. A great cottonwood tree 6 ft in diameter and three big branches is located high
on the rocks. Then for half a mile below the fall the river divides into
numerous channells amid rocks and boulders and makes a wild scene.
We portage the stuff from E's boat to the bottom over a trail we find
above the river 100 ft. taking 9 loads from his boats. Eat lunch and put
up tent to keep things dry as it still rains occasionally. Go back and lift
Edith down to the tree lifting the boat over a small rock, first one end
then the other, put the boat into a corner between two rocks and put
poles across and lift the one end up keeping the bow tied to the tree
from above, get it balanced and then tip it down. Take a picture of the
boat standing on end then slide it down into the water. Tie up as it is
beginning to rain again and we all take a load from my boat and go
to camp.

The river is rising again and is the dirtiest color imaginable. The
mud is so slippery one can hardly stand and the rocks are of a hard
lime formation and slippery as glass. The lower walls are reddish
brown in color, dark, and there is a light colored strata similar to our
blue lime on top. Red cedar is plentiful at the bottom also box elder
with seeds similar to maple. We see no birds but hundreds of dead fish
killed by the recent high water.

We have a comfortable camp high in the sand above the river. The
boys announce supper. All tired.

Drizzle   October 1
Sunday   Emery

Our boats being left in a dangerous position we had to work all day
instead of our usual rest. Jim cryes quite frequent.

We set up a scaffold or brace for skids by the aid of log allready lodged
between rocks. Jim takes moving picture as E & I raise and drop boat

onto lower side. We then run the 2 boats to our camp ½ mile below.
The channell was narrow and water dropped ferociously.
This ended our work with Hells half mile.

Ellsworth **Rain all night clear this A.M. I go up to my boat while E. gets breakfast and pack the boxes down. Then all go back and finish the portage. Take a few pictures and loaf around camp until noon. After lunch we take the M.P. camera up to the rapid and begin to line my boat Jim taking pictures all the time. get it out to the big tree where we build a triangle to keep the boat from wedging had the boat up and down the other side in a short time. Ran the rapid below the falls to the head of the island half way down It had very large waves and was going some I** ~~lost~~ **got my oar out of the oar lock and had quite a time getting it back. was fortunate not to strike any rocks. Emery followed safely.**

Line the boat a hundred yds past the island where the water simply shoots away about 30 miles an hour Emery goes down it and gets out in a second but lands on a rock near the shore signals the clear channell to me and I follow running the entire rapid to camp safely. E follows Clear tonight.

October 2

Emery Cloudy Drizzle

Left camp 11 am. and on 1st rapid I hung up on a rock. Boat turned and cockpit filled immediately. I soon had her off but cockpit being filled I had to land to bail.

Ed warned Jim if he cried again he would beat him so he solemnly got in and worked. In ¾ hour we were off again and by 5 P.M. we had ran 19 rapids and came to the end of Ladore where the Bear Yampa river empties in.

Echo
Park
We had dropped 425 [ft] in 20 miles. We see sign of horses & cattle and are quite certain we are near Chew's ranch.

We find old cabin but Pat Lynch[8] the occupant was not there. Ed makes camp while Jim & I set out for ranch as we wish to send him across country by land to Vernal if possible. We get to ranch at dark and enjoy a good country meal.

Dark when Jim & I get back to camp.

C 20

Start at 11. Strike a rough rapid with a few big rocks just below camp. Emery is floating easily past a rock when a wave lifts his boat and he is flattened out against the rock his boat standing on edge. I land just at the head of the rapid and start down when he gets his boat loose jumps in and rows to shore, the boat half full of water. Jim has a little cry until we tell him what we think of that. We promise to get him out at end of Lodore if possible.

Run 19 rapids in all and get out of Lodore at 3 to Echo Cliffs about 600 ft high. Here the Yampa River comes in, a stream of a dirty clay color and quite large.

We are informed there is a ranch below here and another up on the hill. We find the first and the two boys start out to find it while I stay in camp. They come back at ~~noon~~ 7 having had a disgustingly big meal at the ranch. They report that Jim can go out on Wed to Jensen and take our plates etc. C 20 End Lodore.

Clear.
Chew's boys come to camp. I drop down river in my boat a mile to
cross them for horses. Swim 8 of them. We all take dinner at Chew's. Make pictures of Harry riding bronco. Return to camp take Ed's boat with mine. Pack plates and go back by trail to Chew's so Jim can go out next morning. E & I get back to camp 12.30 AM.

The boys come down from the ranch and Emery rows them across the
river so they can catch their horses. They find 8 and drive them across the river. The current is very stiff as the river has been rising. A little colt places its feet on its mothers flanks. They drive them over a high point and up on our side. We all go up to the ranch for dinner and take some pictures including a couple of Pat Lynch, an old man of 84 who lives at the River. A peculiar character.

We go back to camp and run the boat down to where Emery had left his and get all films and plates (exposed) in a box and go back with Jim. Possibly 60 lbs. Get back to camp dead tired at 12.30. Very frosty and wet.

October 4
Emery

We leave camp 11.30 and immediately drop into some of the finest scenery we have had.

Whirlpool
Canyon

The coloring was gorgeous with folds of jagged rocks sticking up from Boneta bend. We are now in Whirl pool canyon and has a right to the name. With Jim off our minds and a clear day we take a new hold on life even though we are fatigued from our hard work of the night before.

The river drops rapidly and when we came to rapid # 4 it looked to be the highest waves we had met. We ran it successfully as well as 17 others. This was the finest sport of our trip.

Island
Park

The canyon is 14 miles long and we ran this in 2½ hours. We then came on Island park where once more the walls widen out and the sky can be seen other than straight up. The view was superb.

The river here winds 9 miles through these islands to gain 2½ mi. 2 deserted ranches. cottonwoods etc. Water was high which accounted for our progress.

Split
Mountain
Canyon

We then enter Split Mt. canyon which is 8 miles and encounter the highest and fastest waives of all 9 of these we left behind us by 6 pm. Making 27 miles 5 hours.

We camp as it starts to rain. ~~Rained all night.~~

Ed goes over two rapids he did not expect. Goes completely out of my sight. Timing speed of Ed's boat but forget time when he dissapears from view even though I am 10 ft above water. I expect boat to be smashed but was only a large wave and his boat was unharmed.

Ellsworth

Camp 20 in Split Mt.

Take some views and start at 11. High tide. Ran a three rapids with a good current then come to a fourth which would be bad in low water. We take it easily. We get out of Whirlpool at 3 P.M. and stopped 1½ hours to take pictures. Some very big rapids 18 in all and wonderful scenery. Light rocks like pinnacles on top lighter than crossbedded sand tapering or blending to light red then dark red below. Covered with pines on top 2400 ft high, Cedars and at bottom an box elders and cottonwood both with yellow and green leaves. Wonderful folds in the rocks. First part like Cataract. Emerge into Island or Rainbow Park. Wonderful coloring rolling hills purple cream, light red etc. Row

9 miles to make 2½ the river is so crooked. We get through at 5. Enter Split Mt. First ~~Mt~~ rapid big waves and very rocky high velocity next one is divided into three sections with smooth swift water between. ~~I g~~ Very much like a fall. I go first and make it safely Emery ditto. High water makes our first big waves. Ship some water. Run the next without looking at it. ½ mile long and very rapid. I go over the next before I can stop and almost get in wrong. Go over a rock but clear and boat plows away down; out of Emerys sight. Get out safely two more very choppy ones then a very big one. Emery goes first O.K. I follow and get into the bad water. Emery is high up but cannot see me some of the time. Get out without hitting anything. Camp at 6.30. Running time about 5½ hours 26 miles. Stopped two hours to take pictures. Shower. Camp 20 right side under box elders. Big rapid below.

Rain

Just got our tent up in the eve. Wed. when it started to rain. We had easy minds as Jim was off our hands and everything was stored away dry. We slept well and in the morning found it had fallen ½ inch during the night. We allready had a rase of 2 or 3 ft. and this added to it gave a good clearance to the rocks the following day. Though it did make larger waves. Took a moving picture of us boat running the 1st couple rapids (raining).

We enjoyed the continuous descent and kept on successfully running rapids without looking them over.

We ran 14 ~~miles~~ rapids and all good ones in 2½ hours. One, the 3rd from last ran under ledge on right (down)

When we reached the end the formations were carved into grottos. We then pulled hard and struck the dredge about 3 Pm. Ate our lunch in the office as it was raining the door open. Telephoned and found we were 9 mi. from Jensen.

We left the dredge 3.53. Just above Jensen sun set was georgous, heavy clouds hanging over snow capped mountains Everything rosy tinted, rainbow to the N.E. which reflected in the water. Reached Jensen at 6 Pm. Jim had gone through at 11 am. Stayed at Snows al[l] that night.

Ellsworth **Jensen 21.**

We both run the waves of 1st rapid and make some moving pictures Run 14 before we get out of Canyon. Scenery continues wonderful. We get out of Canyon in 2½ hrs. rowing. End of Canyon wonderful alcoves 25 ft under rock. 3rd ~~rock~~ **rapid from end goes under sheer wall. We run it safely keeping toward shoal. Rain when we strike valley. Run 7 miles and stop at dredge. No one there, door open. We use telephone and find we are 9 miles from Jensen. Reach there at 6.15, 11 hours rowing in 2 days from Pats hole, Snows ranch**

October 6

Emery Clear

Secured horses from H.J. Chatwin P[ost] M[aster] to go to Vernal. As we enter the Alwilda a voice fermilliar exclaims "You fellows are the toughest I've seen for some time." It was Duff the Rag Time piano player who used to entertain us 6 years ago at B.A. Hotel.

That night we had a jolification. Jim sang once more. We all sang and the house was filled.

The people all treated us roally each one trying to outdo the other in hospitality. (Mr. Adams of store)

C. 22. We find Jim and Mrs. Chew passed yesterday at 11 for Vernal. We hired horses and go to Vernal. Beautiful farms. Lots of poplars and fruit. Mud everywhere.

Find Jim and an old friend Duff at Alwilda. Shop most of day. In evening crowd gathers in room and we have music. Nice time.

October 7

Emery Fair. Frost.

We get Jim off on stage to [*Words marked through and illegible*] Price by stage. do some shopping and then arrange with D. P. Trim to develope plates etc. in his darkroom. Invited to dance but are too tired and go to bed instead.

Ellsworth **Jim left on stage. Happy boy. We shop most of day and develope our plates at gallery of Delos P[icture]. Trim. Fair success. Too tired to go to dance in evening.**

Send plates home. Films to Eastman.

Beneath the Jensen bridge

Vernal Sept. [*October*] 7. 11

letter from
Emery

My Dear Blanche.-

I tried to wire you from Jensen yesterday but the wires are down on acct. of heavy rains all through this country. I know you will be anxious to get word again from us as we have been a trifle longer than we had anticipated this far, but was on acct. of the extreme low water which was a great detriment. We have had a great trip everything fine and not a pain or ache except some sore fingers and a rough seat.

When we started we used to have some fine songs by Jimmie but when we got into the canyons and running rapids our merriment from him ceased. Each day he grew more melancholy. The farther we went the worse the rapids and the harder the work. When we got into Ladore Canyon he lost his nerve entirely and must thought he would never get out as he would cry like a baby very frequent and always when we hung up on a rock, struck a bad rapid or got into any difficultly. We never let him run any bad rapids but put him on shore. When we got to the end of Ladore we found a ranch where with we were able to secure transportation for him here and he only beat us to town by a few hours. It is certainly a releif to have him off our hands as we thought the trip was going to put him insane. We find we can work so much faster and with the weight of him, his bed and grub gone certainly is a lift. We now have 150 miles of hard rowing ~~and~~ to Green river and if you write do it quick as a little rise is on and 10 to 13 days will likely be our time there.

We have had no upsets. Twice were thrown sidewise on rocks which turned enough to allow water in our cockpits which got into back hatch. Lost our rifle & shotgun in one of these as they were not tied and sank. Our stuff got all wet and it took us a couple days in both cases to dry. Then we have had 11 days rain. We set up our tent and build a fire in front of it. Set up our table, open our stools and we are as comfortable as at home. The scenery in beauty has been beyond any description I can give or ever seen. The trees go all along the river to the top. We have had some hard portages and are very tired every night. I have gained 5 lb. I was surprised to find what a country this is as I allways thought Vernal a little town about like Williams and a P.O & store at Jensen. This is true of the latter but we hired horses and came to Vernal. All the way up we go through ranches as far as the eye can see and could look back into the last canyon we ran. I never saw any where the equal of their apples & fruit of all kinds.

We cannot get sugar so must get hony to take its place. We are certainly getting our feedings and people are treating us so fine everywhere it is great. When we got to Vernal at the hotel a bunch of surveyors were sitting round a table playing cards. One of them said "Well By George you fellows are the toughest we have seen for a long time. It was Duff a tall young curio man at the Hopi house who used to play rag on the piano at B.A. until all the guests from the El Tovar was down to hear him.

Now if you think this town didnt have life in it last night you are mistaken. I never heard his equal for rag playing. Jimmie sang once more. We all had our little stunt and the street in front of the hotel was crowded. We just came up here for the day but was too good so we stayed over night and I am writing this early this morning to get it off on the mail.

I only wish you could be here with me. It is such a fine country. As to the views, I know they look a little flat but in a whole think they are the best we have had and you will find they will sell. Tell Mrs. Smith about us meeting Duff. Say what do you think; we learned that Galloway was along the river some place and saw us but did not make his appearance. Isnt that small. Say nothing to anyone unless you tell Clarence. We are glad not to need anyone. We are sending our plates & films to Green River where we may develope as we do not have time on the trip. It seems hard to keep up even on our daily notes. I am certainly glad E.V. is getting along so well and hope things continue as favorable on that end as they have been. It makes me feel bad to think of that sore throat and think we should tend to it and see the cause.

Our moving picture camera is working fine and we should have some great stuff. We may send 4 rolls to Eastman and see if it can be saved. That which got wet. The boast didn't have rubber on top as they were ordered so we are buying bread boxes to keep our stuff in. Ed has become quite an expert oarsman, but one has to develope something coming through what we did.

This town has two banks & many stores all more up to date than Ariz. B R.R. towns. Tell Edith I named my boat for her and she gets some pretty hard nocks some times. I think of you both all the time and will be fine when the trip is all over and we can be together again. I mean so I can make it again. Well dear with lots of love I am Your loving husband

Emery

Fair. October 8

We go back to Jensen and enjoy the farms with irrigation ditches and Emery
much fruit. Get to Jensen 6 P.M.

**Lazy A.M. in P.M. get our horses and go back to Jensen. River has fallen Ellsworth
one foot.**

Fair October 9

Leave Jensen 11 am. Small raise on the river but stick on sand bars Emery several times.

Noon just above Alhandria where we meet Mr. Stewart prospector who had informed ladies of our coming.

Mrs Johnston insists on us accepting 3 jars of fruit and a little butter. We camp at a mining proposition, the only one we have found working of the numerous ones along the way.

Ellsworth **Start at 11. Eat lunch at 12 Strike a ranch at Alhandra. Prop. wife very nice to us. Gives us fruit. We pull hard and reach gold dredge in eve. Boss in town. Camp ½ mile below dredge. Emery has been feeling bad all day. Goes to bed same C 23**

October 10
Emery Cold

Leave camp late. During night heavy wind with rain came up. Ed gets up and covers things up. I am feeling bad on acct of too much to eat at Vernal but get over it after the night passes. See many ducks & geese. See Indians.

Ouray
Utah Row until dark so as to reach Ouray. Wiered scene of squaw peering through trees just above Ouray.

Got meals with storekeeper.

Ferry. Indians Uncomphographies sent in from Colo. also Uintas.

Ellsworth **Heavy wind & rain last night. I got up and held things down.**

Go over to dredge and take picture. Row all day against a hard wind. Reach Ouray late in eve. See some Indians. Get supper at Mr. Currys of Merc. Co. Sleep in our own beds at ferry. 24

letter from
Emery   Ouray, Utah, Oct. 10, 11

My Dear Blanche-

We have a little rise on the river and are making up a little for lost time. We left Jensen yesterday afternoon and tonight are about 80 miles nearer Green River. So if we continue to keep up this pace we will be there in 8 or 10 days. You did not say in your letters if you got my letters from the following places. Linwood, a ranch near Red Canyon, Bridgport, Ladore. We are glad to be alone as it is much easier and saves so much time. This is an Indian res. we are at now and we were glad to get here for supper. The country here is great with the bottoms filled with cottonwood. I wish you could see it as we do.

The people arround here have certainly been fine to us. One lady along the way yesterday ~~have~~ insisted on us accepting a 2 qt. jar of peaches & plums and a 1 qt. jar of picklelily. Civilization was a little too much for me at Vernal and I had a little spell last night but am over it now. We have both been fine.

We are beating Stones time now but on acct. of the low water in the start he went much faster than we.

We are sending in your name the plates we developed at Vernal. Keep them in a good place. We will develope again at Green River. Our moving picture films we have sent to Eastman to develope. Tell Earnest to save a little of the blond for me.

Love to all and a big kiss for you and my little baby.

Your loving husy. Emery

Leave Ouray 10.20

See many Geese. Country much similar to Browns Pk.

Cannot assertain just where canyon starts in 1st part simply cliffs on one side and then on the other.

Cattle everywhere and trails on both side.

Color of cliffs burnt sienna & grey. Very little vegetation.

Make good run and camp 2 mi. above ferry in head of canyon. Just about sunset when… of rocks…bushes…add forms…f……object. I discovered what appeared to be a deer with large …the water…ing last… The only thing I thought of was to get a moving picture of him. I still was not able to see if it was a deer or not. Ed called to look at …deer. I grabbed my motion…a and… another deer but…jumped from the island. I hope the film gives somewhat of an idea of this picturesque sight. [*This page of journal is irretrevably smudged*]

October 11

Emery

Take a short moving picture of Ouray as we leave. River sluggish. Dueschne & White come in. Muddy. Cottonwoods everywhere. See pictured rocks. Take photo. pass dredge. Noon at begining of cliffs. Walls go from one side to other. Lots of cattle. Camp near where we think Stone did.

Ellsworth

Scare deer from Island and he jumps into river. E.C. take moving picture. Late. Beautiful Island edge look like trimmed hedge. Dark red brown, yellow & green. Yellow trees in centre. C 25

October 12

Emery

Clear.

Stayed in camp till 3.30 After arranging our boats we started down the river and were soon at another ferry. Here we met a cowpuncher but did not stop even though he invited us to stop and eat. He asked where we were going and on informing him threw up his hands and exclaimed "My God! Well boys its yours, I hope you much success."

We ran until late and could not find a suitable place to camp so had rather an uncomfortable place to throw our beds.

We saw many geese through the day and quite a number were squacking on an island just beside us.

During the night I was wakened by something which sounded like singing and when I was fully awake found it to be coyotes. It was not the 1st. time I had been wakened by them but on this occasion I will never forget it. Seemed that one persisted in reaching one note higher each time and what made it so strange & beautiful was on account of the echo vibrating from the walls. I wakened Ed to hear them who agrees with me as to the beauty of the music.

Ellsworth

Work all day at our boats rearranging boxes etc. 3.30 start down River. Two miles below pass ferry and 1 man invites us to camp. Decline. Hear wagon near creek. Hundreds of ducks & geese & mud hens.

8 mile run. Camp at bend in wall. See comet. Clear & cold. Camp 26.

October 13

Emery

Clear

Broke camp about 9 am.

Desolation Canyon

The walls were beginning to close in on us and we were well into Desolation Canyon.

While the 1st. part of the canyon is well named I do not approve of the name being carried down the whole 97 miles as from the middle of it to the end is one of the finest of all the series in scenic beauty. Innumerable forms of every coceivable creature could be seen with the use of very little immagination.

There was more vegatitation and cattle could be seen occasionally.

We ran 13 large rapids & 13 small rapids reaching Range or Rock creek just at dark. This was a clear beautifull stream.

In the canyon at last. Ducks and geese every where quiet water. Walls Ellsworth
getting high. Strong wind to row against but good current. Lash both
boats together at noon and drift with the tide. See a great arch on West
side. Short distance below see our first rapid. In afternoon run 13 large
and 13 small rapids.

Friday 13, Camp at Rock Creek. Same as Stone. Heavy waves and
good current best run yet. Late camp. Camp 27.

Clear. October 14

The canyon ~~grew~~ walls grew higher and still more picturesque. We Emery
ran many rapids and some of them bad ones. 12 before dinner. The
1st. one we stopped to examine before running, made quite a roar. We
found our boats had been landed on the wrong side to secure a position
for examination and even though a stiff current prevailed we decided
to cross to the west side. I landed with ease and seeing Ed was having a
little difficulty called to him some advise. He did not understand and
stopped rowing for about 2 strokes to listen. This was just 2 too many
and we both saw he could not land and must be taken over the rapid
without knowing anything of a channell.

I called as he passed me and told him to be carefull of a large rock
I could see in the high waters while crossing. A point projected out in
front of me so I could not see what was ~~going to~~ happening.

I ran as best I could to get a vantage point and on reaching it he had
passed the rock and was drifting down sideways in the big trough of
waves and he could not get his boat head on but the swift waves soon
had him at the bottom without mishap.

To avoid this bad rock I pulled far to the east side and was well out
of danger from the main body of water. However it was a stretch of no
little importance that had to be handled carefully and for all I had seen
a sumerged rock the current threw my boat on it. The bow was thrown
about 4 ft in the air but soon settled down flat. I threw my weight on

the side that was fast and thrust an oar in the water which threw her bow down in the stream and with a few light bumps I was soon at the bottom.

The next large rapid had very heavy waves probably the highest up to that time. I ran it bow first and had the peculiar sensation of nearly being thrown backwards boat end for end. Crossed oars look like fish tail to Ed.

See large natural bridge on mountain.

We see many cattle along the sides and a made trail for them. At 4 P.M. saw a fine looking ranch and stopped for information. It proved to be James McPherson's a cattle raiser. A large swing suggested the man was a home man and on meeting him found him of the best western type. He invited us to spend the night which we did.

Ellsworth **Start at 9.40 Run 14 rapids in A.M. 9 of them good ones. No. 10 very heavy opposite a beautiful park on East with large square rock in center. Heavy waves throw boats around like ten pins.**

In afternoon we run 10 rapids. One looks bad and I go over as usual without intending to. Wave carries me straight for big rock near shore. Wave sends boat through channel only 14 ft wide then it turns around again and drifts side ways and all I can do will not straighten it. Emery takes other side and turns on a rock but gets through. Another splits 3 times. Emery takes one and I another. High waves where they meet but no accidents. Last bad looking rapid has a rock ~~channel~~ bar clear across very bad looking and we get M.P. Camera out. E.C. takes me first as I take left channel very easy. I take him as he comes getting him from below.

McPherson Ranch **At 4 P.M. pass ranch and stop. Mr. McPherson asks us to stop and we do so. Three boys here also, very plesant company.**

Camp on Florence Creek just below where Stones party was ~~wrecked~~ upset.

[*A note at the top of the page of this entry states* "**Mr. James McPherson, Elgin Utah. Ranch at Florence Creek.**"]

October 15

Emery Clear.

Not wanting to spend a day extra with McPherson we did not hold up as usual on Sunday and started down the river. The 2nd large rapid below his place was a bad one and decided to make moving picture of it. Ed went 1st. and ran it so successfully the picture will not show much.

If the camera had been on the scene in my run a little more excitment might be seen of dodging rocks however no damage done.

We discovered we were approaching 5 men in a boat. These men proved to be doing work for a dam which is to irrigate thousands of acres of land around Green River.

They kindly invited us to stop for dinner at their head quarters which was a mile or so below. We accepted as usual. The dinner was prepared by Mrs Steel and the pie not being passed the 2nd time gave no chance to reflect on our manners.

The rapid at their place though full of rocks we ran with out examination.

We continued on and accepted an invitation with Mr. Wilson whose ranch is at the dam just above Green River 7 miles.

Mr. Wolverton's son being the one who took us in.

Up to this place Hells half Mile was the last line or portage.

A.D. Wilson Ranch at dam above G.R. Utah.   Ellsworth

N.E. Wolverton, G.R. Utah

Run 18 rapids for the day besides lots of riffles & shoals. 3d one below Mc P. is Chandler Falls and the creek is opposite. Natural arch is on left 1800 ft. above. Run fall safely. 12 ft drop.

No 6 is a rough one take it safely. This is in Gray Canyon. Des. ends 3 miles below McP. Meet some (5) men from dam (Buell) who ask us to dinner, below very bad rapid at dam site worst for day conclude to run it before dinner got over without looking it over. I go first. First channell is good but lots of dodging. Full of rocks. Finally get in a nest but only strike once, no harm done. Emery hangs up for a short time but gets off. 17 ft. fall in ½ mile all rocky. Land at Boarding house at bottom. Dinner.

Several very high wave rapids below dam 121 ft fall in 26 miles to G.R. Ship water in high waves 5.30 strike dam. Stay for night.

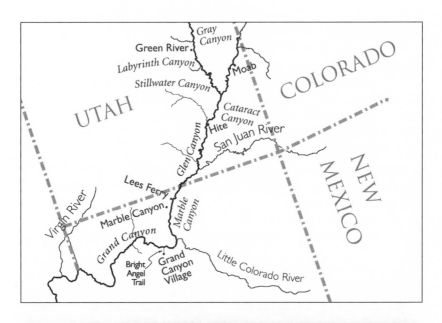

Filming in Cataract Canyon

Green River, Utah to Bright Angel Trail

Made a let down over the dam. Pictured Mr. Wilson's house & water wheel. Left about 11 and was in Green River in 1½ hours. Left cameras and boats in charge of Yokey. Developed some plates and films. Put strips on boats.

Stay at the Metropole Hotel.

Get news in Ass. Press.

Stay until friday.

October 16 through October 19 Emery

C 29.

Take pictures at Wilsons place. Line boat over dam on right side Easy Leave at 11 Reach G.R. at 1.30. Leave boat with Capt. Yokie at pumping plant. Hunt up Mr. Woodruff friend of Wilsons. Make arrangements for developing etc, Stay at Metropole

October 16 Ellsworth

Green River, Utah Oct. 16 1911

letter from Emery

My Dear Girl-

Sent you a telegram this afternoon of our arrival which I suppose you have by now and likely glad.

Well dear we got all the money at both places.

You asked about Ladore. Well we were in 10 or 11 days rain and had it mean that way but the meanest of all was poor Jimmie who lost his nerv and cried. You know Ed & I don't bother about a little thing like that as rain. We have had no upsets but two tilts in which the water gets or got in our cockpit then ran into the other compartment and did some damage to everything. Probably 4 rolls moving filmed damaged some.

Lost two guns. Have had much excitment but have not seen anything that scared us very long at a time. Say dear I wish you could have been with us from Jensen down.

We were invited to stop with one rancher the 2nd day out but it was too early in the day so we moved on. Before sunset I took a moving picture of a deer leaping & splashing accross the river after we passed him. We camped late. Next day we camped at a beautifull side stream.

Next night with a rancher who had some of the finest peaches & apples you ever saw. He was a cattle man. Next day nooned with a government irigation party. lady cook, lemon cream & O my. Ed's getting fat. Next night with rancher at dam 7 mile above here, and now I'm in the dining room.

The people have certainly been the finest on earth and we surely appreciate it.

We rec'd. letters from Galoway so things don't look so bad. We will try and keep in the limit of this $100 you sent us so not to have so many notices come in on you. We are going to take our boats out and go over them tomorrow, and do a little fixing which the people in Racine did not do.

We have a man here who is interested in us and is taking us to every party we wish to do buisness with and is very nice in a strange town. We have lots of work here but will try to get out on Thursday. We have 110 miles smoothe water before entering Cateract and then hope to be able to send you a letter out some way and let you know how we get along. We went much slower than Stone in the upper Canyons but from the last day in Ladore have beat his time ~~before~~ by several days.

It will be close to a month when we get to B.A. but before we leave here we will or I will give you Stones time from here to B.A. but you must not worry if we are a little longer for we are going out to the natural bridges. You never say whether anyone is interested in our trip or not. It is certain the people along the way are.

I just hope we get through with out loosing our boats but that is an easy thing to do. The worst bump I got was in quiet water.

When at the canyon I have wondered if the cottonwoods would ever cease coming down the river but I know now they will not. They are simply immense. We are not worrying about you not doing enough dear or much else except getting through. We are ~~not~~ sorry not to receive some of our rope postals we asked you to send us but as he spoke about a package there may be the cards are there. I will see in the morning.

Now dear I know you and Earnest lack a little as to information of what we have gone through. From Green River Wyo. We have passed through about 9 canyons. Over 400 miles and dropped in elevation just 2000 ft. of this drop 420 ft is in Lodore or part of it say 12 mi. We will now go through Hell roaring Can. Cateract can, Glen Canyon, Marble, Grand, and Black Canyons. The drop form here to B.A. is 1544 ft, and from there to the Gulf 2436 ft. You might copy this for reference.

I guess I have written enough tonight and think someone is waiting on me. I hate to think of going past Indian Garden Camp and not finding Spauldings there.

Give every one our regards and I am glad to know Edith is such a good girl. I had my picture taken with a little girl yesterday away up in the canyon.

Love to you and baby and if there is any over give it to the school teacher.

I know the time seems long but it wont be so long.

Em.

October 17
Ellsworth

Pack goods and unpack express, see newspaper, get boats out etc. E.C. developes a few films etc.

Wednesday
Green River. Oct. 17,11

My Dearest Wife.

Here is another day gone and nothing done but hard work. Ed developed some plates while I put our boats on dry dock and put ~~on~~ some oak strips over seams which <u>they</u> should have done. They put some on but not enough. The strips certainly save the bottom of the boats and we were pleased to see they were in so good shape as they are. We had intended to develope all our films here but we have so poor accomodation that we will likely send them to you and develope ~~until~~ when we get there.

We took dinner with a German woman tonight and it was fine. I just can't get enough to eat. I just gave my grocer order for the trip to you. While I think of it there is a P.O. at Hite so you may try to reach me there, it may get there before I pass. We do not look for as much trouble below as we had in Ladore, but one cannot tell. The 11 days of rain made it hard for us. We have our boxes here which are supposed to be water tight.

Yes dear I get lonesome to see you all but I just throw it off. I know how much harder it is for you at home than the one away. This is a very little town but I wish you could get some of the good things to eat in fruit etc. and everything is cheap. In regard to Earnest we would be glad enough to keep him if he fixes it with the folks.

Say dear wouldn't you like me to rub my nice beard on your face it is a peach.

We will have a couple hundred pounds we will freight from here home, over stock of plates and things we can do without.

When you write to Hite tell me if much interest is taken in our trip. Did Lindy come back. We wrote to Rust. We find about all of Cateract Canyon can be walked. (Goodnight from Emery)

We expect to leave here tomorrow noon…

Emery works on boats I develope plates.

leaving day.

letter from
Emery

Green River, Utah Oct. 19, 1911

Dear Blanche:-

Emery is in bed and I thought I had better drop you a line... I think Emery says you are worrying because buisness is not what's the use? You know we don't care as we expect it at this time and if the buisness is not there you can't make them buy. I'll give you some-thing real to worry about. Emery can't get enough to eat. Fact. We are getting our meals at a boarding house run by a German woman who sets the best table you ever saw and half an hour after he has eaten he will be sneaking around to a restaurant for some pie & coffee and such like. I never saw him so fat. We could not get away to-day. Leave tomorrow A.M. early. We have been tinkering on the boats putting oak strips on the bottom which was to be done by the factory, but was not and other little preperations.

I was under the impression that the Denver bill for shutter was paid but suppose I am mistaken. If you have last months statement where you can see it you might look it up. The bill for case of plates and the two to Abercrombies should be paid at once if possible.

Don't let the books worry you. Figuring is always hard and the easy way is to sum up the cash once a week and divide it up for the week. It certainly does take money to do this sort of thing.

This is the first place where have not had to get someone to cash a check and we are going to keep what we have with us as it is cer-tainly inconvient to be without it as we have found. We are sending our films and plates and a lot of stuff including two cases unexposed plates to G.C. More bills.

I suppose Emery told you that as far as we were concerned Ernest has a job. The only thing is to get Mamma's consent. She told me when I was home she did not want us to take here last one away.

Glad to hear you are getting along so well. The weather is a little cool to-night and we will be glad when we get into the Canyon's again. We only have 40 miles of rough water in the next 320 which means hard rowing, sticking on shoals etc. as the water is low again. The high water certainly made it fine for us. The news papers, al-ways on the lookout for something sensational has made as much as possible out of our little tilts and makes them look real thrilling but there has not been anytime when we did not feel master of the situation and posed for pictures in the worst rapids. This is the place where Russell & Monnett, Stanton & Brown, and the Best expidition started. They did not get the benefit of the experience of the upper Canyons. We have descended 2000 ft. and it is only 4000 ft from here to the coast and we don't expect near as much trouble below as there is more water. We had a hard time of it until after the rains. I don't know whether I will want to go back to the Canyon or not after this. I suppose everyone I know has left and I think I will apply to Galloway as an apprentice.

We wish we knew if we were getting anything with the Moving Picture machine but we will have our trip and won't have to tell tourists that "we intend taking the trip someday."...

I hope you don't have to work too hard. Take things as they come and don't worry.

We hear Hite is a P.O. Hite, Utah. Write there at once and let us know how it goes.

Lovingly your brother
Ellsworth

Green River Utah
Oct 20 1911

Dear Blanche.-

We did not get off yesterday and are just finishing breakfast to leave now Friday. We have got quite a load and have to take a couple fellows several miles so don't expect to make much time. As to when we will get home you know how things go. My opinion is a month but I would like to get there for Thanks Giving. We can write you from Hite and give you probably a better idea...

Well we see the papers are giving us a little advertisment.

We hate to leave the good cooking but then we have a nice layout ourselves. There is a thin sheet of ice this morning and we will be glad to get in the canyons again.

We will try and make the bridges but don't be dissapointed if we are not to you in Nov. 15 or 20th for we must make the pictures as we come to them.

Now be a good girl and Edith also till dad comes marching home again. With love and kisses to you both I am your own little boy.

Emery

The *Coconino Sun* ran a front page article 20 October 1911: news item

MAKING PERILOUS JOURNEY
Kolb Brothers Write Last From Jensen,
Utah, on Way Down Colorado River
A postal card dated at Jensen, Utah, from the daring Kolb Bros. photographers, who have undertaken the job of securing moving pictures of the Grand Canyon from a boat, was received by the Sun this week, which says:

"We have had a successful trip thus far in our boats. Plenty of excitement, but boats still riding dry. Our third party would weep like a child when we got into tight places. We sent him home 155 miles overland to rail. We two will continue trip alone.

Kolb Bros.

The fact that the Colorado river through the Grand Canyon has never been navigated but once and then in specially built boats made for Major Powell by the United States government, will give a person some idea of the perilous undertaking. It is ten chances to one that this card may be the last ever heard from the intreprid adventurers.

October 20

Left Green River and took R. Woodruff and Ingrem down the river   Emery
about **20** miles. No rapids. Low hills of grey, brown, pink, red, & yellow principally grey.

We landed at Wolverton's **4** P.M. but decided to camp with him for the night and met several surveyors who helped pass a pleasant evening. Wolverton was one of the best men for information of value we had met.

Ellsworth [*Words written on back of page.*]
Stereo.
#2 Canyon on west with 3 alchoves.
4 I. fort
6 Shelving rock 10 miles
8   "   "   below Wolvertons
10 Natural Bridges 1/22 [f] 16
12   "   Arch   "   "
3¼ x 4¼
1 same as stero 2
2 twin alcoves.
3 ledged rock.
4 hogan arch
5. looking down noon
6
7
8 Looking East at bowknot
9 2 spoiled
10
11
12 Looking West at bowknot.

October 20

Ellsworth Left G. R. 9.00 A.M. Mr. Woodruff (Harry) and Engermann on board. H. W. in E.C.'s boat helped row. went with us about 20 miles to Dellenbaughs Butte. San Rafael just below. Low cliffs either side.

Dellenbaugh Peculiar purple color in rock light yellow sand, pink cliffs, Dellen's. Butte Butte dark red above gypsum Pink below. Get to Wolvertons at 4. Stop. Engineers came down in eve. Bed 9:30 Cold night. Camp 31.

October 21

Emery Left camp after 9 am. and soon were into the walls of Labyrinth Can. These walls while low are beautifully carved and the canyon well bears the name.

Many bends in the river at sunset we camped just below the hogback on the upper part of the bowknot.

We decide to spend the next day here also for Sunday.

Leave W's 9.30 Take photos through Labyrinth. Walls principally light   Ellsworth
& dark red, seal brown, Indian red, pink shades, light rock on top.
Walls from 125 ft to 300. Get off and take photos natural arches. Indian
fort from boat. Camp early on North side of bow knot. Bacon, eggs &
cocoa with bakers bread. Camp sand and chaparrall willows on edge.
Clear and cold night.
   Height of walls about 700
   Temperature. Night ice, Noon shde 54 Sun. 102. Water 52° C 31

Clear & beautifull.   October 22
   Climb up the hogback and take a view of the bownot. Carv our   Emery
name with penknife in the soft red sandstone.

Snappie air crisp & clear. After breakfast we take kodaks & climb neck   Ellsworth
of bowknot conclude we want large camera and I go back for it. Take
two plates of center and one of either side also small ones. noon. Paint
***"Defiance"* on boat. Temperature water 52° C 31**

Clear   October 23
   Arise at 5 am. Leave camp quite early. Stop at turn of bowknot. climb   Emery
wall and make views. 50 minutes took us around bowknot. Distance 6   Bowknot
mile around. 1200 ft accross at nearest pt. Walls become more interest-   Bend
ing and forms of rock still bear resemblance of every living thing.
   Pass Hell roaring Canyon with out knowing it. pass 2 tents Get out of
canyon and see butes of the cross. Camp right on river.

Up at 5 Start at 7.48 but only got ½ mile and climb the hill for pictures.   Ellsworth
Lose 45 minutes at this. 45 minutes to row around loop [*illegible word*]
& tiresome run Slightly cloudy Current good. Emery misses an oar
from his boat. Noon at Hell Roaring Canyon and I lose an hour try-
ing to find D. Julian's name[9] 1836. I do not find it. Eat lunch as we drift
with the tide. Rocks cut into wonderful shapes sheer above bright
red slope beneath usualy dark red, light gray flinty rock beneath and
peculuar blue green walls which round off like elephants backs. Top
formations splits into fingers 400 ft. high. Pass two tents on flat. Call
but no answer Run 2 miles farther. Camp on right just out of canyon.

New bushes on border. Small dark blue berries elongated dissagree-able taste. See lots of large willows. Climb small mound and see buttes of cross in S.W.

Emery is not feeling very well retires early. Night clear quiet quite warm Bed 9.45.

Pictures Stereo. looking across dividing ledge at loop, fingers on loop. Diana fingers at gate looking west. Camp 323 just out of Labyrinth on right of Buttes of Cross in sight

October 24
Emery   Hazy.

Make turn of mile or two, then climb up short distance to picture butes of the cross.

River then makes a curv bending directly east for several mile with only thin wall for partition. Walls with lone standing rock carved in peculiar shapes were still ~~more comm~~ numerous.

The walls now were the walls of still Water Canyon and closed in more than that of Labyrinth. [*illegible word marked through*] Still water was true enough but Labyrinth might have been carried into it as the artitectual curves were just as plentifull. There was little vegetation ex-cept just along the banks where willow grew in profussion.

We lashed our boats together and drifted down as we ate our lun-cheon.

Stillwater   In the afternoon the walls grew higher & higher and the peculiar
Canyon   forms gave us much ammusment as we passed by them.

We saw Happy Hoalogan, ladies with Merry widow hats School rooms with its occupants and any thing of life that is common place.

At 5 P.M. I see a place that looked to be fit for camp but not just suit-ing us we go on a little further. We kept on & on but still we could not even get a good landing. At one place we see the dim forms of ladders high up the sides of the red wall and here make a trial at landing so as to picture the ladders and the ruins of the dwellings but the bank was so steep we had to give it up. We finily find a rock were we land and tie up for camp. On climbing up the bank see the track of men of recent imprint. Also the little flat above just beside the wall is the ashes of a recent fire with potato pealings near it. As yet we have no idea of who they may be. (Bees on willows[])

Morning slightly cloudy, warm.

Ready to start at 8 but only run a mile and spend two hours photographing Cross so call it 10 Pass tents and building against cliff at Bonito Bend three miles below camp. Belong to G.R. boaters. River swings East very sluggish. Got into canyon of wonderful rock formations. Red below with a hard flinty lime on top, red weathers lime projects back from river peaks run up to great heights all shapes draped figures larger than Liberty statue domes & temples, arches, cathedrals, tunnells, caves & grottos farther along lower strata is dark brown and red in rounded formations of smooth surface, reflecting the sun. A Biliken on a throne with a thousand worshipers bowed around him, no stretch of the imagination to see every person of note reproduced in rock a mar spectecled school marm, a street scene with all persons wearing Tam O Shanters, animals of every discription and geometrical figures of without end. Canyon deepens and wall go up on either side straight, we round a great bend where our maps tell us Stone's party lunched. It is a little early for us to camp although the situation is good. A few cedar trees dot the hillside which begin to slope part way up. The banks are steep and muddy and we can not see a suitable place to throw our beds. We row down slowly searching both banks. My brother who is behind discovers some ladders leading to a small cliff dwelling high in the rocks. Thinks we should land and examine them on the morrow.

I have a long pull back up stream against a current which I had thought stagnat a few minutes before but now call a hard one. Land to find it an unsuitable place, no wood, no level ground. Reluctantly give up the dwelling and take to the boats just before dusk a mile down stream we find some rocks fallen from above into the river which affords a landing. We quickly climb out and find it to our liking. A level place 20 ft above the river with a straight wall at our backs. A few fallen rocks show us what might happen but we risk it. Discover remains of a camp fire mans shoe tracks three or four days old.

Menu for the day Fried corn meal mush, comb honey, coffee, cornflakes. Noon hot coffee, veal loaf chile sa pickle lily, bread butter honey, apples. Eat as we drift. Supper Cheese omlet, bread tea.

P.S. We find Whimmer's boat on West bank about 4 miles from last tents where river turns south, bow sticking out a short distance. Tie white rag. Opposite a small Canyon two rock formations chimneys 200 yds below on east side 50 ft above largest cottonwood tree.

Camp 33.

Emery   Clear & murky

After 2 hours run we are in water with more descent, whirls & boils and know we are near the junction of the 2 rivers.

See canyon a mile up where Dillenbaug & Powell climbed on top. We camp on the west side on large sand bar and decide to climb on top to the split rock country. Make early lunch and work our way up the river into cut where we climb the 1500 ft. wall. On reaching pictured Stantons name. painted ours at junct.

Camp under pretty willow.

Confluence of Green and Grand (Colorado River)   The top we were astounded by the magnificent view. Our first view accross the country may be compared with looking from N.Y. to Brooklyn at the church steeples as there were hundreds of pinacles. The rocks were split so that we would step over crevaces with hundreds ft depth below. We look into Cateract canyon. Make stereos & 3¼ views. A little chipmonk the only life we saw.

Get to camp at 4.30. Find beautifull fossiles & crystals.

Ellsworth   **Warm Slightly cloudy.**

Made a two hour run on a good current with numerous stops and reached the Junction. Water in Grand has been very high and has more red color than Green about same amount of water. We eat an early lunch then take our kodaks and walk up stream about a mile to a side Canyon or break where we climb out. Take a picture of bend in river like Capitol. View on top takes ones breath away. Peer through crack and see Colorado below 1300 ft. and great mass of rocks everywhere like fingers. Spend three hours taking pictures of views of canyons and rocks. See snow covered mts in East. Mts south and West. See about 3 miles of Colo. River. Lots of cracks between large rocks. Principal color of rocks red white below main Canyon like Cataract reddish white below. Find pink and yellow fossels & crystals. Coming down in boat pass swarm of bees feeding on yellow matter on willows.

Back to camp at 5. Dried beef stew cocoa and fried pototoes put us in good humor. Cloudy warm. Storm brewing. We load M.P. camera, fix hatch cover and bake bread.

Camps. Leave G. R.
Friday 20. 11 Wolvertons.
Sat. 21. Bowknot
Sun. 22.   "
Mon. 23 End of Labyrinth Cross
Tues. 24. 6 miles Junction
Wed. 25. Junct on top
Thurs. 26. Smiths camp M.P.
Friday 27. Rapid 23.
Sat. 28.   "
Sun. 29   "
Mon. 30.   " 32
Tues 31
See loose leaves Nos 14 to 26 [*in Ellsworth's supplemental notebook*]

Sprinkling.

October 26

Ed. takes picture as I pull the boats into the junction of the 2 rivers. *Emery*

About 1000 ft below we get the effect of the two joining with rushing up stream currents, whirls & boils.

Find we are in a different class of water and run very rapidly. *Cataract*

Run no 1 on left side. *Canyon*

Sand and hard rowing enlarged oar locks and both oars pull out for the 1st. time as I run No. 2. both get through safe but ship water. No. 3 is as bad as the 2 just passed and my oar locks coming out again causes me to drop on a rock but not to hurt boat. Ran No. 4 easily.

No. 5 has the largest dip we had seen and looked bad. Ate lunch and set up cameras to snap while running. I make moving picture as Ed ran both boats through. Ran on West side. Ran onto camp about rapid 3 where boat had been tied and fish caught.

Appears to be 1 man & dog.

We pulled our boats on shore and walk down to examine No. 6 When we turn to get our boats I saw *Edith* was loose quite close to shore. I run but she was out too far to reach. Could easily swam to her but thought *Defiance* was right there. Instead she had come loose & floated down through some bad rocks 100 ft or more and when I get *Defiance*, *Edith* was well under way for the rapid.

I climb in *Defiance* and pull with all might head on down the rapid and while I caught up to *Edith* I was going so fast I missed her. When I gained controle I jumped on stern to grab her but caught my heel in Edd's hatch falling crosswise on my back. Would have plunged backwards head on in the water only the heel held me. *Edith* was now headed directly for large bad rocks in rapid 7 so I row ashore and ask Ed to get in and we follow. He thinks best for me to go ashore and runs 7 on south side. *Edith* plunged and rocked going through the rocks with out even touching though the channell curved every way.

Ed catches up and is now in a whirl pool. He crosses for me. I was completely exausted from my row & run that I had to rest a little. Had not been feeling right since catching cold at G. River.

We keep on and run No. 8 easily. (Rockey). Then we shoot down swift water and soon turn into large park with a few trees.

Shoot at ducks & miss.

Then we run 9 & 10 & 11 & 12 with out looking at them from shore point our boats bow first and pull down the swift water [*The words "ship water" were added as an afterthought*] Happened to glance on shore & see a camp. We land and meet Mr. Smith who had left G.R. on the 5th and was trapping & hunting on his way to Needles in a shell of a rotten boat which Yokey sold for Galloway the builder.

Smith was small wirey. With one eye out. An intelegant cleanly sort of fellow. He knew nothing of what he was up again and was scattering all his camp stuff out to dry just having an upset or his boat filled with water. Had as much cool nerve as I have seen. Objected at first to having his picture taken, then gave in.

Said he hadn't done anything but was sensative about his eye.

What we thought were dog tracks were coyotes. We camped and had him eat with us and seemed to enjoy some pineapple, the last canned fruit we had.

In the morning he rode with Ed a couple miles down to watch us run some rapids as he could get his frail boat over by lining only.

Our camp last night was under a weeping willow tree a beautiful camp
and protected from all dew. I crossed to op East side of Green and
painted our name on a rock and took a photo of Stanton's record etc.
also our boats at the Junction. Had a little sprinkle of rain at our start
a good swift current started us sailing down the river but ¼ mile the
waters of the two mix with a great turmoil and whirlpool the Grand
appearing to be the higher of the two. Possibly 2½ miles down we
come to our first rapid. It is much like some of our upper ones when
the high water was on but greater force behind it. Long interference
waves. Emery leads, I follow both making it safely keeping on the left
or South. No. 2 is larger and tails out with big waves for ⅓ mile. Take
it on South. Both ship water. Emery's oars come out of sockets and
he rides the waves. This happens in No. 3 also and he strikes a rock
after he goes over a dip. No 4. is easy above then a little rougher below.
Pass it easily. No 5 is the biggest yet. Large square rocks on the South
and most of water going over dip waves possibly 7 ft high and curl
back nearly all water going to a tumultous center. There is a channel
on the other side but we eat first. We started at 10. Stop at 12. Get M.P.
Camera & 8x10 out and Emery makes pictures as I run through. Make
it safely but it is 3 P.M. before we are ready to push on again. We have
been seeing quite fresh tracks on both sides of the River and what we
take to be dog tracks, also can see where boat has been tied at no. 6.
We have pulled our boats up on sand partly and are tw 200 yds below
and on coming back see Emery's boat float down on the water. Emery
runs for my boat while I follow on shore thinking it may drift in. It
gets in swift current and passes close but can't reach it and it goes for
three big rocks about 25 ft square with a narrow channel very crooked
between the boat is carried safely through riding high and touching
nothing. Emery has run rapid on other side but fails to make it and
gets close to boat but current carries him past. He has climbed out on
my front hatch and gets his heel tangled up in some sticks which I have
put over hatch to keep cover on, and nearly falls into water. He is too
close to another rapid to be hampered with boat and comes to shore
for me. I take boat while he runs down shore. Waves carry boat into
middle of great bad waves full of rocks and it reels and plunges and it
seems as if it must be smashed. I run South side in clear channel and

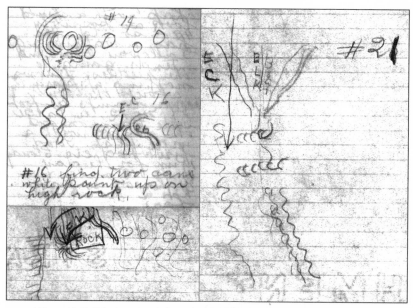

Ellsworth Kolb's drawings of rapids 14, 16, 21, and 22 in Cataract Canyon

gain a little on boat but it catches in a big whirlpool and the run is over and I paddle along side and get the line and tow in. Emery, who has not been feeling well, is quite exhausted from his efforts, and complains of pains in lungs but keeps on. No 8. is quite easy but has a lot of rocks, but we swing clear.

After this a quiet stretch for some distance then we come to a wide open park at the end of a side Canyon with some cottonwood trees. There are some ducks on the river and E shoots at them but without success. Below we come to No. 9. a clear drop then some swift water for 150 yds. and another rapid. This is a big one but we run both without getting out of boats. The channel is quite clear of rocks but water is heavy. We both ship some water. After this we have about 3 miles with only one little rapid then another big one. We have run this one and are turning our boats bow down stream when E. calls and points to some boxes and camp articles and we see a man at work on shore. There is a boat near by. We land and introduce ourselves. Mr. Smith is evidently hunting and trapping a little and has had an upset and has all his stuff out to dry. We can sympathise with him. He is a small man one eye out of a light sandy complexion and hair and mustache. Is a quiet sort of chap with a shrewd look an possibly 42 or so old. He has a water logged Galloway boat and intends going to the Needles. Knows nothing appearantly about the River. [*Charles F. Smith*]

We camp at foot of No 12, a large side Canyon on the South with a wide flat. Good fire wood etc. Cloudy. Run for the day 11 or 12 miles. Neither of us have hit a rock so far.

October 27

Emery

Rained all night & ran in our beds. Took Smith over 2 little riffles then let him ashore to see us run No. 13 he is much interested and says my boat just looked like a high bucking bronco. No. 14 is a little worse. He helps us in a little moving picture. I take E. as he runs both boats through her. Night before he speaks (S.) of the water being trickey. We bid him good by. No. 15 was easy. Ed said he had looked over 16 and follow him. I did but he had not looked over it very carefully. Got in a little worse than he. Went stern first over large rock, dropping into a back swirl. The back wave was so strong it through me again the combing taking both oars out of my hand but they were tied. I got ducked the water breaking all over me.

Mile
Long
Rapid

No. 17 was not a bad one and we ran over easily.

We gave considerable study to 18 large rocks had rolled clear accross the river I made 8x10 of Ed running thi 18 was big but we ran it with ease.

No. 19 not bad. No. 20 divided by island. I find bottle with name & request to write to sender. We run this one on the south side and is like Ladore. We both hit rocks on the bottom but slow velocity did no harm.

No 21 was a mean looking one. Ed runs in large center channell and is completely swamped in waves. I snap 8x10 of him but is dark and may not get it. Then I run down to see how he gets through as projecting rocks obstruct view.

I pick out another channell but as I am dry and Ed is not he takes my boat through the channell I picked and did not ship water.

#22 on first sight looked like a hard line or portage. bad rocks. About 30 ft from shore and immense rock divided channell. Water ran up on it for many feet then simply dropped on either side.

I ran it clean and took but little water. As Ed was hurled like a dart almost on top of the rock, then dropped into the immense curl I paid too much attention to him.

My bow was down and saw I must let it strike square on a rock near shore. Ed was swamped and passed by the bottom of the rapid having difficulty to land on having cockpit filled to seat. He came back and helped me swing into the clear and was here an accident might have happened.

I could not swing as quick as I should from a rock and in my effort got a trifle sidwise. There was two back curls which flooded my boat and sprayed or dropped all over me. Just as I caught my breath to take another stroke I discovered my block where my oar socket is held had split both screws and socket had gone. Anticapating just such acci incidents we had tied another oar lock beside the first. The block was not split bad enough to prevent me from making a successfull landing just before being carried over the head of as bad a rapid as we have encountered and where I am now writing.

We pulled on the west shore where the walls are sheer but do not run up until some distance back from the river. We pitched our tent and stretched a line to dry the close wet from the rain while camped with Smith.

We find boards enough in drift to floor our tent for both beds and as it rained all night enjoyed our tent.

Ellsworth **Rain all night ½ inch.**

Took Smith with us over 2 little whirls which we did not count. Put him on shore and ran #13 big water, strong waves no trouble. Pool below and tail.

No 14 full of rocks channel on West or North turmoil and a whirl where all force poured into a hole 4 ft deep below rock. Get Smith to help us get moving picture. #15 over easy. #18 [*possibly an error probably meant* #16] is one big dip Emery loses hold on oar and clings to boat no waves below #17 easy #18 immense rocks on steep sides so came on bad channel lots of time lost. Photos #19. Easy #20 run after lunch divides on Island lots of fall like Lodore Rapids take left channel each rap a

few rocks no harm done find bottle with request for finder to write to Miss Minnie Koppe, Delta, Colo. Ah Ha, a romance at last.[10] No 21 is a whopper, biggest waves yet like a little Niagara, rocks on either side but appearantly a clear channel. Prepare for picture. Box canyon on North or right 100 yds back. Sheer walls 1600 north side South sloping. Cold and cloudy.

I take my boat down the V into the heart of the big waves, mount the first but the second curls over on to top of boat half fills it and turns it around I dip into a couple more but land safely bail out I am soaking E. C. is dry so I run his through but keep out of center in choppy waves and get through with no trouble. #22 a sheer fall at beginning lots of rocks with a large rock 20 ft, nest north from shore, and a clear channel through waves current runs up on large rock which slopes then backs and divides. Emery runs on with current backs and shoots through clean. Boat whizzes through possibly 30 miles an hour. I follow but my boat turns bow first and plunges into whirl at side of rock, then sticks its nose into the big waves 5 ft high and fills within 1 inch of seat. I drift down very heavy and have hard pull to shore Emery is on shore above and I help him off. Camp.

The Big Drops

Rain. Camp in sand under sheer wall on right. Large drift piles fresh from last raise 20 ft above river. Find pumpkin. Put tent up by rock stretch line and build 5 fires and dry stuff which had gotten wet from rain & full boats. Bed 11.

Rain.

October 28 Emery

Wake up and see clouds settled down in the canyon and a slow rain is on. I have been feeling bad for some time so decide to keep our dry camp and stay until Monday. Had fine success at making hot cakes for breakfast.

We look over the rapid below and come to the conclusion of running it knowing we will get soaked but think it clear.

Rain all night. Emery feels badly and we do not move camp do a few odd jobs E.C. puts name in white paint on wall head of rapid 23, 450 ft from river. Night clear sky. E.C. no better.

Ellsworth

October 29   Clear
  Emery   Stay in camp all day.

  Ellsworth   **Same camp all day E.C. some better. Clear.**

October 30
  Emery   Left camp at 11 Am. Both run #23 and I was glad to get over with out shipping much water. I still felt under the weather and very weak.

Drop in 23 is about as much like a fall as any we have seen.

E's boat ships water to the seat.

#24 is clear but large interference waves & I ship much water. 25 not so bad. 26 not serious. Canyon more open. We land on S. side at mouth of canyon where there are a few nice cottonwood trees and lunch.

#27 Divided in 3 parts the 1st. 2 rather swift and the 3rd. very large waves. Ed & I both ship water and land. Some of the waves were extremely high and on standing at top or bottom our boats would apparently go under the water as they were hidden by waves. Then came some swift water which we dashed into and was great sport. I would have enjoyed it better but was very weak. We were trying to catch up to an oar Ed lost above swept off while running a rapid but we cannot get it. 28 & 29 not hard to run. No. 30 a little worse with boulders to dodge. #31 not so bad. All these waves splashed water enough to cause us to stop and bail. 32 good descent & swift but we get over safely. Not feeling my best we camp early.

During the day on the left saw name of A. G. Turner painted then still below the name Socialism 1912.

As there were Cliff Dwellings above the name he apparently is going back to the Aztecs.

  Ellsworth   **Lots of packing to do. Got out M.P. Camera and took pictures of each running #23 big waves, bailing etc.**

We also have a 5x7 showing height of fall much like a dam descent about 10 ft in first plunge. I half fill with water. #24 is clear with big interference waves. 25 smaller 26 small turns sharply to right against bank. Last two are in more open canyon. #27 just ahead at noon very large whirlpool and swift water above. Emery very weak. We are at mouth of wide Canyon with cottonwood trees, on left side, noon.

The Brave Ones

Taking on Big Drop Three in Cataract—Kolb's Rapid #23

Rapid is divided into 3 sections last one biggest drop, very swift water and we are flooded below this we have 2 miles of the swiftest water we have seen. I have had an extra oar knocked off the boat and we never catch up to it. Current must be 5 or 6 miles an hour.

#28 much like last one 29 ditto but smaller each in 3 sections. 30 is beside a canyon coming in from S.E. Much time is lost by climbing over immese boulders to look the rapids over. A few large boulders are in center of no 30 but we miss them but both of us get drenched in nearly every rapid. 31 is smaller, still water between and 32 is a big drop with a large open space on the left or S.E and a small canyon. We camp 4.15 Both very tired. Canyon walls sharp turn to West below Camp.

October 31
Emery

Rapids 33, 34, 35, 36, 37 ran in morning. Swift water, narrow canyon.

Tied boats stern to stern. I straddle bow and take M.P. picture while Ed rows down stream. And she bucked over 2 little rapids. 38 & 39 were big ones. #40 a bad one.

Then comes 41. We looked over it and while it looked ugly we decided to run. The drop was imense and rocks on the left and middle must be avoided. We start with E about 100 ft in the lead. He drops out of my sight as I take the shoot, then with one slap I was carried into the heavy waves. It was the worst I'd encountered and my boat was nearly submerged on several plunges and one wave let me drop on a rock but Eds oar pulled out. I hold to boat. no injury. We were caught in a whirl at the bottom so landed and bailed out, the cockpits being filled. On the left or east side we saw ladders put up to some cliff dwell. ruins. #42 We were now at dark Can. and see a rapid with island in cent. Water rushed on both sides to shore under shelving rocks and would be death to loose controle of boats but we dash through successfully. The walls are sheer and rapid must be run.

#43 is the last rapid we count and as we are in sheer walls continue to travel though it was fast growing dark. The water was very swift and the scenery extremely exquisit though too dark to photograph. We get to a large bend where a canyon came in on the left & camp by moon- light. Caves in cliffs.

This is the end of Cat. canyon and we feel proud not to have lined or portaged.

Rapid #33 small beginning long interference waves in second section. #34 V & int waves. 35-36-37 heavy water but easy, noon in a quiet stretch. We have had some very swift water in the morning also some very nar- row canyon. Put 2 boats stern to stern and I rowed while E took M.P. over 2 little rapids we did not count. Name A.G. Turner on rock. Three more rapids each one of them big ones #40 a bad one swinging to right shore. Both boats go over safely keeping to left. #41 is a nasty rocky one stream on rig left ladders against hill. See Island [*The words* "Dark Canyon" *inserted above line*] below. 10 minutes later we are out at the bottom of the rapid have just bailed out and man Oh man wasn't she a good one. I went first and missed the rocks I was on the look-out for but dove time and again so it seemed boat must surely be standing on end and blinded by spray. In the last one my oarlock pulled out and I had to place oar against my knee to get a pull most of the pulling had to be done with the other oar as good fortune would have it.

Emery got pulled into the very middle of the big the waves and for 4

Dark Canyon (margin)

Ellsworth (margin)

dips was completely hidden by spray which came from all side. There ~~was~~ were a thousand waves each jumping a different way. The rock formation at the bottom is hard & sharp. We see a sort of cliff dwelling above the river near the ladders (White mans). All aboard for 42 It does not look so bad from here but at the Island below we look for hard work.

Ran #42 without trouble & a little one below we do not count or look over. Emery is ahead and keeps going. Island has large line of rocks to left and he goes to right. Is surprised to find the current on right ran against the wall with great force. I snap a stereo of him as he goes over.

This rapid can not be lined as walls are sheer 75 or 100 ft on both sides. We pull hard away from shore and keep out. Current then swings to left shore and we cross the big waves and repeat the operation. We count 43 rapids in Cat. We now have a run through very swift water and keep going until dusk. At 6 oclock we reach a large Canyon coming in from the South and camp at the end of Cataract. Large level spot. Caves.

Ran a little rapid and then rather a stiff one to begin Narrow canyon, but was the only bad one in the canyon. The water was swift and the walls narrow being about 1500 ft high. We called and the sound would travel or be heard for a long time. Echos etc.

November 1
Emery

Narrow
Canyon

Photo Henry Mts. & know we are near out. We come to the Dirty Devil then tie boats together and eat lunch. Stop at log hut. Then tent where we find miner (Kimble). Then drift down and glad to get mail at Hite P.O. We write all afternoon. ~~and next morn.~~

Hite
Utah

Run a small rapid at end of Cataract then go over a large one at head of Narrow Canyon, the only one of any importance. We have very swift water and travel fast and the walls quite close together but not high. We see Henry Mts. from Canyon and take photos looking through also one looking back, longest straight Canyon we have seen. Take picture of mouth of Dirty Devil stop at tent a few miles below and find a Mr. Kimball, three miles below is Hite. P.O. with John Hite in charge. Spend afternoon writing and sleep in cabin.

Ellsworth

Nov. 1st 1911

Dear Blanche.

    I guess you will be glad to know we have just arrived at Hite. 2.30 P.M. We have just had the finest success any one could ask for. Have ran every rapid in Cateract and hardly touched a rock. *Edith* and the *Defiance* don't show what they came through. Yesterday we certainly rambled. Came through some of the worst of all rapids. Our boats leaped and plunged like bucking bronchos. You can feel pretty sure that you will see a camp fire in B.A. Creek from about any time after the 15th. Can tell you better from Lee's Ferry.

    We have found out what our boats will do and where there are not rocks will ride any kind of water. One of Stones boats was left here and in comparing them find to be a frail craft in comparison. Hite just now said You boys certainly have the best boats ever put on for the trip and I've seen all of them but Powell's. We are glad some of our film sent to Eastman was saved as we thought it would be lost. Our new boxes keep everything perfectly dry and our cameras are just working fine. We feel proud of our success in Cateract as there was some angry rapids. We are extremely carefull always having our preservers on, and then we know our boats can't sink, so just keep on with your good faith like you always have and that only a dear brave wife could that we will come out with a dry deck.

    We have not had the least kind of bad luck since in Ladore but we have had much excitment and certainly for sheer walls, arches, domes, towers and a wicked river, Cateract is beyond Grand Canyon. What pleases me most is that we are this far and everything is OK. with you all. Just think by the time this reaches you I will be in a land where we can both look at Greenland Point. You on one side and I on the other.

    We ran on a fellow in Cateract just drying out all his stuff. Only in the head of the canyon. He was a man used to rivers but had no idea of where he was or what he was up again. He had a frail boat with quite a load and lined what rapids he went over as his boat was open. We offered to carry him through but he refused even though we told him of his perdicament. There are rapids and miles of canyon he cannot get over in his shape and though he promised faithfully to write, he will never have the chance I think. I never expect to hear of him.

With our boats we are having just the right stage of water to make a successfull run.

I am glag there is a P.O. at Lee's Ferry. Wish you could have Reed or some one camped at the end of Hances trail to make a moving picture of us running the Sockdologer rapid. When you see the big fire down in B.A. creek let it be known the same evening at Hotel. It will be in that little place where we turn the glass and we will sort of clear things up in our boats to run to the trail the next day.

I have got to be quite a cheff and you aught to see some of the dishes I get up.

We have certainly lived fine and our camp stuff is just right. Ed and I get along dandy when we haven't any one else to bother with. This is a sort of little ranch right on the river and just out of Cateract below the Dirty Devil.

Well dear I don't know anything else to tell you. O yes I dreamed I was with you the other night and it was fine to have a warm bed fellow (Thats all). I would like to get hold of Edith and give her a good hug. Tell her if she is real good and minds you I will come to see her in a little while.

Well for this evening good by. This goes to you in the morning.

Love and kisses from

Emery

Ed is writing Stone.

You pay the Eastman Bill and tell them to ship the negatives and posatives at once Wells Fargo.

Leave Hite at noon. Swift water. Take stereo of cliff Dwell's. Pass Lopers ranch. Running little ripple as Loper hails us and goes accross with us to Cas Hites John Hite's brother.[11] He was just coming in from his gold claim. Has a unique little ranch in a pocket with pretty brook running by.

Loper who is Miller (?) Herbinger's 2nd. immediately brought some melons from the celar as well as delicious grapes and apples. Had a nice visit and left his place about 10 next day.

Pish La Ki

November 2
Emery

Red
Canyon

Ellsworth **Leave at noon and pass Bert Loper's Dredge, 1 mile below his ranch. No one at home. Pretty spot. Some distance below hear call and land. Mr. Loper joins us and we go across to Cass Hite's Ranch. Beautiful spot. We spend the night and enjoy hearing the old mans reminiscence Navajo chief great friend of his. Navj. name Hoskinini Pish La Ki. Loper tells his side of story. Tick-a-bo.**

news item Front page, Coconino Sun, 17 November 1911:

DARING VOYAGERS HEARD FROM AGAIN
Kolb Brothers Reach Hite Utah—Find Stranded Man Who Refuses Help—Will Try to Reach Bright Angel About Nov. 15

Hite, Utah, Nov. 2,'11.

Editor Coconino Sun:

Arrived here yesterday eve.

Boats and cameras came through Cataract Canyon successfully.

One boat got away, empty, plunging over two rapids before we recovered it. Each of us lost one extra oar.

Heavy waves tore oars from our hands on several occasions. So severe is this jolt that the oak for oar locks were split. Another socket and extra oars have prevented serious trouble quite frequent.

The 10th Rapid in Cataract brought us upon a lone unfortunate man whose tracks we had seen above.

He was on shore with all his grub and clothes strewn around after being swamped in the rapid we had just descended. His frail, open boat could only be lined around the rapids.

We offered our assistance in reaching Hite and even though we read to him of Powell's and other trips, he refused any aid. He was absolutely ignorant of what he was into and will surely come to the same end as dozens of others have with such a craft.

Two parties last year started in Cataract and have not

been heard of and with such a boat as his the heavy waves will knock it to pieces in the first rapid he is compelled to run. Only a few miles below him, the water simply drops, sucking every drop from the shore, then hemmed in by sheer walls, plunges over a steep line of boulders. Having successfully made the upper canyons, we are now on the stretch where Best, Brown, Stanton, Russell and many others attempted. Stanton's, Stone's, Powells and Russell's parties being the only ones getting through. They all had their boats destroyed before reaching Needles.

We leave for Lee's Ferry today and providing success expect to reach Bright Angel about the 15th inst. We will then continue to the Gulf.

Very respectfully,
Kolb Bros.

November 3
Emery

Before leaving, Cas hite gave us more fruit than we had had for some time. That night we camped in a little building in connection with the ruined dredge that Stanton had.

Took photos of hireogltphics.
landed.

Glen
Canyon

Load up on fruit and leave at 10:30. Noon on boat. Reach Stanton's old dredge in evening. Camp on opposite side at small building. Dredge a ruin.

Photo hierogliphics.

Ellsworth

Start early and have swift currant.

Flat country turns into canyon again. Pass Escalante River. (deep gorge.) Cannot find camp so keep pulling in the twilight until moon comes up and we find ourselves at the San Juan River. Pull accross and have a wiered sensation as strong currant sweeps us tward dark cliffs with little chance of finding a landing. Camp opposite San Ju.

November 4
Emery

San
Juan
River

Get an early start and go with a good current. Get out of flat country into canyon. Pass Escalante river at 3. Farther down photo a rock with

Ellsworth

four openings like face. [*Ellsworth used ditto marks under* 'openings']
1½ ft diameter, all connected. Red sand rock. Do not find good camp
and pull till moon comes up. Get to mouth of San Juan. Seems to
be large stream swift current can't land at mouth. Water carries us
swiftly to the black gorge of Colo. where moon light does not enter.
Wierd sight. Land on right and find good camp, scarce wood but we
rustle enough. Bed at bottom of sheer wall. I bake bread.

November 5

Emery   Ed gets up early. Leave 7.15

We search in canyons for Howlands and Duns names.[12]
Unsuccessfull.

Walls of arches, domes, ampetheatres, all kinds of artitectual forms.
We pass the canyon to natural bridge before knowing it. Then pull
down stream. Wind blows hard but currant is swift. We try time and
again to land for camp but find none. It is just dark when we do get a
landing but camp is not the best.

Ellsworth   **I make a mistake and get up early Start at 7.15 to get to Navajo Mt. Look
in several Canyons for names of Howland & Dun. Fail, but take pictures. Farther below we pass the Rainbow Bridge Canyon but do not
know it and hunt for hours drifting farther away all the time. Heavy
wind blowing up stream but current down is the stronger. Finally discover where we are and get in and pull for a down stream camp. Camp
on north side near small creek at Ute crossing.**

November 6

Emery   We find in the morning to be just a little above the Crossing of the
Fathers. Climb up about 800 ft. Hear pounding and blasting in the
distance.

Leave 9.30 and are at Warm Creek before noon where we discover
the pounding was the building of a steam boat for the Gold Co. at Lee's
Ferry. Dan McConvill formerly at Grand View is here.[13] Take dinner
with them and pull at 1 P.M. pass Navajo & Sentinel Creek. Walls deep
& red. currant swift. Land and eat supper at Dredge Lee's Ferry a[t] 5.15
making 35 mile in 4 and ¼ hours. Rust had waited on us 2 days pulled
out 1 day ahead.

Lee's
Ferry

Climb up rocks on South and look for a way to get out. See Mt. away Ellsworth behind. Start at 9.30 Get to Warm Creek before noon. Find outfit building steamboat. 17 men Dan McConville a miner whom we know is here.

Take dinner with them. Pull away at 1. Anxious to reach Lee's Ferry before dark. Canyon gets deeper. Pass Navajo Creek on ~~right~~ left. Later Sentinel Rock. Take photos Canyon finally breaks and slopes and at 5.20 we get to Placer Camp at Lee's Ferry. Find Rust left day before, left letter at P.O. Eat supper at camp.

Load films repair oars etc. write letters. November 7
Emery

~~Breakfast~~
Ellsworth
Meals at camp. Put up tent in stone bldg. and load M.P. Camera and plates. Repair boats etc. Cloudy P.M.

Lee's Ferry Nov. 7 11 letter from
Emery
Dear Blanche.

We got in here last night at 5 P.M. Got a little past the place to go out to the bridge so decided not to go back and kept drifting. I was dissapointed on not receiving any mail here from you and as there is a mail coming in today we decided to wait over and start tomorrow morning which is just 2 months since we left Green River Wyo.

Rust was in here and waited 2 days. Left for Kanab the day af before we got here.

We had a good run from Hite here. Nothing unusual. I am writing from my boat which is tied up to the gold dredge. It is a buisy place with about 25 men at work. Looks funny in between the hills. Some Johnston boys run the old ranch and you aught to see the fruit. I now look up and see the fort which John D. Lee[14] built while in hiding from the soldiers. I am still in hopes we can reach B.A. about the 15 or 16 watch for a fire in B.A. about that time but don't get scared if it don't show up for there are so many things that may hold us up 3 or 4 days longer.

We are tinkering up our boats a little here.

They are building a good sized steam boat up the river and when we saw it looked like that mith land ship you and I read in the magazines about. Ed says to look for a fire on the 4 14th but don't get dissapointed. We are getting our meals at the boarding house and since we left Green Riv. I think my cooking is the best we have had.

An old timer is sending with me a couple bunches of grapes & apples for you and baby. They are turning to raisens but are certainly fine. I may eat them myself. We rowed over 50 miles yesterday but now will go slower on acct of rapids.

We are 161 miles from Flag and by river to you about 110.

Well I'll save the rest of this till I see if I get a letter from you. This is the last sheet of paper I've got.

Well the mail has come and you did not write so this is all I'll write.

You must be awful buisy that you could not write your only bunch of garlic.

Ed sends his love and I don't know whether I should or not but I will anyway. Good by From

Hubby.

November 8

Emery We left Lee's F. about 9. am (cloudy) All ~~whole~~ inhabitants could be seen as long as there was no obstruction ~~strait~~ distance Then a long but not dangerous ~~small~~ rapid took us around the corner out of sight of all human life until we get to B.A. trail.

Badger Creek Rapid We ran three ripples and then about 5 miles below come to Badger creek. This was a good stiff rapid but we ran it safely. We then drifted on, the walls becoming higher and about 4 P.M. got to Soap Creek rapid. This is evidently the worst bad rapid we had seen, for big water.

Soap Creek Rapid After carefully studying over it decide it can be run. One large rock on the right. I set M.P. camera up to take E. as he runs his boat through. I feel a little weak in the nees as I see him begin to descend into the monsterous waves. I keep turning M.P. E. makes one deep plunge and is then carried to right by rock. He pulls his best but too late the stern hits her. She does not stick but the recoil is so strong the boat is upset. E. holds on and she rights herself and plunges down the frightfull descent. He lands and we bail.

Our waterproof box was not proof and we spoiled some films & plates.

E. thinks he knows the chanel now and says he will run my boat through but for me to be ready in case any thing happens to get him.

The walls are deep, beside it was well on to 5 P.M. and I ask him to wait until morning, but he wanted to have it over with. He was some time getting started and I hoped he would give it up till morning. I started a fire so he would not pass the landing on acct of the darkness then I watched. The wind blew hard and Oh! how long it seemed.

I watched carefully and at the top of the rapid I saw the boat: then it dissapeared and in an instant I saw the whole boat in the air. It dissapeared again, and I waited and watched but could see no sight of her. I was possibly ⅓ or ¼ mile below the head of the rapid. There I stood with his boat ready to catch what might float down. Finaly I saw a dark object speeding down. I pulled Eds boat loose and saw it was my boat upside down. But where was Ed. I rowed out and heard him call what I thought was "Let her go." but as his boat got near me I found he was calling to catch his life preserver which was floating ahead of the boat and he was clinging onto the *Edith*. He called to get the life preserver so I would think he was all right and so I would not get excited.

The boat turned with him on the upper side so he was out of my sight and I still had some ~~worried~~ moments of worry before his boat ~~was down to~~ reached mine ~~we rowing~~ I was pulling up stream and he drifting down. When she neared me I made up my mind if I ever did any thing right I must do it now as we were fastly drifting to a curve in the river where the rapid which carried Brown[15] under the cliff. As *Edith* came toward me I grabbed her bow then I through Ed a rope and told him to let go the boat. I pulled him ~~beside~~ to me and with my right arm under his tried to get him in. I could not, so I dropped the rope holding *Edith* and pulled him into my boat. Then we took after *Edith* which was darting one way and then another as there were many boils and the currant was swift. When we got her she was well on the way for the rapid and so heavy we could not do much in the way of a landing.

Ed said "Now Emery keep your nerve as we are being drawn into the rapid where Brown was drowned. I saw the overhanging ledge in front of us and put every bit of strength I had ~~and~~ as well as my knowledge of pointing the boat in such a turn where the currant goes to the wall. E was holding the rope of the capsized *Edith* and as we swept by the wall he said "Good Boy. now let me take a turn." I did but still the current swept us on and another rapid was passed. E said "We will turn her loose if you say the word." But I did not instead of saying it I took hold of his oar and pushed as he pulled and we did land her in a whirl.

We camped on a large high sand bar, using my bed which was not very wet. His bed was left at the foot of the large rapid with about 200 lbs of other luggage after his first tilt.

We had not lost much and thanked God our skins were saved.

Ellsworth **Camp 46.**

Take a couple snaps of stone bldgs of Lee's and view from his lookout on right of river on top of mound. Start 9.15. Crows follows down River to see us over first rapid. It is a long one, medium waves and slow, no importance, #2 & 3 are small, #4 is the Badger Creek Rapid a fall of 18 ft. in 22 ft. rather rocky at the start and big waves. I go first get my channel and go through but get drenched. Emery follows closely touches a rock and gets his boat turned around and has considerable difficulty when his boat hits side ways against rapid. Gets through safely. 5 miles below we come to the famous Soap Creek Rapid. We conclude it can be run and E sets up moving picture machine 150 ft below first of fall.

The channell is on West side but must miss a large rock against which most of the current seems to strike. I get start all right and run almost clear when current carries the bow of boat against rock and boat is on edge in an instant and I am thrown out but catch edge and pull myself in as boat swings clear and turns up right. Cockpit is half full but I have little difficulty the rest of the rapid.

Find my waterproof box has turned almost over but is held by side straps and has 3 in. water inside. We hurriedly get the stuff out and try and bail out. I propose bringing Emery's boat down although he would rather wait till morning as it is 5 P.M. He stays on guard at end of rapid in my boat while I go up and get his ready. I tie oars securely fix life preservers around chest & neck and put on rubber coat. It is growing dark fast and I make a hurried start. In the gloaming I am a little confused in the direction of the current and quicker than thou[gh]t I am carried over the high dip in the center of the river and hurled at the biggest wave. The boat mounts bravely but is caught and hurled like a feather when the opposite wave strikes. My brother said he could see the boat seemingly entirely out of water and then could see it no more for 150 ft. The first thing I knew I was sinking slowly although the life preservers had a tendency to keep me afloat. I had hold of the right oar and it was slipping down with my weight towards the blade through the ring which was in the oar locks I wondered if the string would hold and felt a great relief when it stopped and I pulled myself up and caught the gunwale of the boat. I was under the boat which was upside down and ~~we were~~ was being carried down at express speed over the big waves. All this happened in possibly ½ minute.

I got my head on the outside of the boat just as we mounted a wave that looked 12 ft high from my low point of observation. The wave broke and gave me a jar on the side of my head I will remember for some time, and after that kept as low as possible. When the waves got smaller I got up as high as possible so my brother could see me and felt reasured. I could see a fire he had built but it was now almost dark.

We encountered more big waves and I got down again paddling with my feet in order to keep them up clear of rocks. They seemed very heavy and cold and it seemed as if the end of the rapid would never come.

I called to Emery and he answered. My neck life preserver had become detached and was floating a short distance ahead of the boat. I told him to get it before taking me in which he did but could hardly see it at first. He then pulled for me and tried to pull me in while he held the boat with one hand but found he could not do so so let go of boat and helped me in then caught boat. By this time we were at the head of small rapid where Brown ~~and 2 others were~~ was drowned. I knew of it and cautioned my brother to keep cool and be carefull as we were still dragging my heavy boat upside down behind us* I tried to turn it over but could not do so. He (E.) pulled with all his might set his oars and kept clear of the rocks under which the current ran but his strength was failing. Feeling better I then took the oars and pulled as we drifted possibly a half mile peering through the darkness for a landing. We finally came to a whirlpool and after a hard pull landed both boats. We bailed out ~~and~~ built a big fire and changed clothes hurriedly. We smell a peculiar odor and think it may be the man who was drowned at Lee's

Ferry some time before but find later it is from a green cottonwood tree which has become water soaked.

*In going through rapids the upturned boat was ahead pulling us downstream.

November 9

Emery Immediately after breakfast we took my empty boat and lined it as far up the river as possible and crossed to the other side. The Walls were high and what shore there was large fallen rocks some of them 75 ft in length. This required much hard work and about noon we had all the luggage carried to the boat. In 5 minutes the swift waters carried us town to the new camp where we set up our dark room and spent the balance of the day developing some wet plates, part of which we saved.

Ellsworth **Spend the A.M. lining the *Edith* back to up the River* and portage the material which had been taken out of my boat and get it on to boat and down to camp. Noon. P.M. Put up darkroom, develope wet plates and load M.P. Camera. Same camp #46.**

*opposite shore from camp.

November 10

Emery Left camp 11 am. Not long before leaving several rapids behind. We had hard up stream wind

Walls were sheer grey on top red and then of burnt color next to river. Very hard no vegetation no animal life. We heard a roar in front of us and looked as though could not sand to view. Try climbing over but unsuccessful ~~find landing on left~~ Find a landing on left. *Edith* nearly got away from me. ~~during the day while looking over a rapid before running it saw mt. sheep dead in the water.~~

At 4 PM we came to a rapid which roared like the Soap Creek rapid. We tried the safe way and lined *Edith* down in 1 hour. She got under a rock in one place and in others was swept again rocks like waves from the ocean. The wind howled and threw spray and sand in profusion. We thought we had a shelter for camp in a canyon on the right. Sand blew in our victuals. We went to bed and little was the amt. of sleep that night. Rocks were blown from the cliffs from above and it seemed the noise from the rapid as well as the furious wind fairly shook the cliffs. We could not had a more miserable camp except it did not rain.

Get a late start 11 A.M. Rapid #8 is rather rough but easy #9 at a small stream on ~~right~~ East sheer walls and bad approach. Land at begining of rapid just around turn of wall at head of rapid. Find it is a big dip over one rock ~~and~~ large waves I get wet. E. clear. #10 at canyon on west rather bad, some rocks. I touch one and swing bow down get through clear. E takes center and gets soaked #11 a six foot drop. #12 easy, below this we come to the large rock fallen in center of the River. We spend ¾ hr. taking pictures. Next rapid #13 is a very narrow channel and a big drop and while it is possibly no worse than lots we have come over the big waves have taught us a lesson. ~~and~~ We line E's boat and take the load up a small side canyon and camp. Ellsworth

We have been pulling against a heavy cold wind all day and seem to be protected here but when we are ready for bed the wind shifts and blows up our canyon and between the roar of the rapid and the wind and covering up to keep clear of the sand have a rather restless night.

We thought the pounding *Edith* got was bad so decided to portage *Defiance*. Had sand and not much rock. November 11
Emery

Rolled her up about 30 ft above water and about 100 ft down river. Ate lunch and left at 2 P.M. and by 4:30 P.M. we had left behind us 9 rapids of which 7 were rather mean ones and might have swamped us. The days being short it was advisable to camp at 4.30 as we were at the head of a nasty rapid. #23. North
Canyon
Rapid

Walls were shere below. The rapid had one bad drop but not rocky. Springs ~~gushed from~~ trickled from the left and we found a marble cave about 35 ft. above the river. Cave
Springs
Rapid

Here we leveled the sand and carried our beds. We were tired but I made several flap jacks and a big pot of hushmagundi.

We were glad that sunday was a day of rest and thought we neaded it.

Camp 48
Ellsworth

Conclude to portage my boat instead of lining it. We have clear sand by going possibly 20 ft. above the water so we get rollers and fly at it but it takes 2½ hrs to get boat below to *Edith*. Start at 2.20 and run for two hours.

Portaging North Canyon Rapid

Rapid 13 is passed #14 is large but safe #15 & #16 do not amount to a great deal #17 & # 18 compare well with Cataract. We run them all. In #19 We both fill our boats and Emery strikes a rock and gets turned around.

Hard work and cold air and water. E is rather protected with the rubber coat.

Pass large canyon on left, possibly Stone's camping ground #20 is just at lower edge and is big #21 is near a small break on left and has a bad approach for landing boats. We get in whirlpool at edge. Discover a dead Mt. Sheep floating in water. This rapid is rather difficult but by doing some neat work we both get through. #22 some smaller.

We are so cold and wet we conclude to camp although we have only been running two hours. We have been seeing lots of lime stone caves and finding one 40 ft above the river beside #23 we camp. It is entirely to our liking 8 ft high and 14 ft square and a sand floor that can be shoveled to fit our beds make seats and have shelves for our material.

Lots of drift wood on the rock below and numerous springs seeping out of earth in canyon just above (West side) Conclude it is an ideal place to spend Sunday. We found a great deal of marble of many hues mixed with other rock.

November 12

Emery

Our marble cave out look was directly over the rapid below but in spite of the roar we had a good sleep and did not get up as early as usual. Ed is cooking dinner and I am now writing by a fire we built in the cave and hearing the angry roar of the rapid we must run in the morning.

Rather cool but we spend a plesant day by building a fire in cave, writing cooking & resting. Marble C. has very narrow channels & rapids.

Ellsworth

November 13

Emery

Well we are over #23 and it came up to our expectation.

We threw sticks in to determin the current and they fairly flew, then with a dive would come up about 15 or 20 ft after shooting through the back wave. Being a bad one we did not try to photo each other running her but thought best to keep close together. E went first and I was just at the top of the shoot when I saw him hurled and tossed. Thought sure he would upset. In an instant I was in the splash. My oars were hurled again the combing nearly smashing my fingers on both hands. I grabbed the boat as I thought she was going over and the water broke my tie on one oar, then drove the handle into my mouth.

When we got through the worst of it I grabbed my extra oar as one was gone with oar lock. I soon had my imergency lock in place and was on the way for the floating oar. I picked it up but prooved to be one of E's he too having the same difficulty or ~~worse as his lock broke~~. We landed & bailed and was off again in another hour. other than a bleeding lip we were as good as new. #24 just as big but better channell on East. 25 small V #26 big V. current on west wall which was clear. 27. 28 all ran quickly. #29 Vasay's Paradice. Made moving pictures.

Vasey's Paradise

Walls open up into butresses, arches, domes, windows, etc. Water in beautifull shreads gush out of wall 100 ft above river. Made move. picture.

30 not so bad. 31 a dandy Ed broke lock here.

Heavy drop large waves. About #30 come to arch and palace.

Marble canyon rapids

1, long, below Lees Ferry.

2 & 3, small ones.

#4 Badger Creek. Bad.

#5 Soap Ck. Capsized.

#6 curv again wall where
    Brown was drowned. Our
    camp below.

#7 a big V. #8 rough, 9 as
    stream

Looked as though no landing
    could be made but we
    landed on the east. could
    not land if water was
    higher.

Ed. touches rock. I clear.

#10 Canyon on west.

11 six ft. drop #12 easy.

13 a big bad one. Line Edith
    Portage Defiance.

#14 heavy waves 15 & 16 small

#17 & 18 heavy drop larg
    waves

#19 large. bow down & cut [r
    or v]. then swing stern 1st.
    #20 below

large canyon on left. 21 bad.
    Find dead Mt. Sheep at head
    of rapid.

#22 heavy. 23 one big dip &
    splash. Springs come in
    on west

We camp here in marble cave.

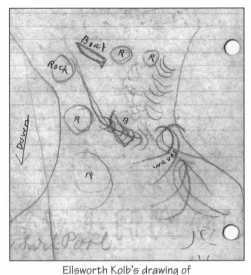

Ellsworth Kolb's drawing of
Cave Springs Rapid.

A day off at Cave Springs Rapid.
Journal in foreground.

Windows caves etc.

Camp in beautiful grotto on west.

Start 8.15. Clear & cold.

I go 1st into #23 shoot down 50 ft. on a smooth drop fastest water yet. Ellsworth Plunge into combing wave and come within an inch of upsetting grab sides. Boat rights and I find left oar gone four strong pieces cord line broken pull with right oar into whirlpool E. follows and loses one oar cuts his lip and bruises both hands. He gets my oar in swift water and rows down stream. I look in whirlpool for his Give it up. Find it later ½ mile down. #24 just as big with a better channel. Run through on East. #25 a small V #26 ditto. big Sheer walls both sides.

Take photo 11 A.M. Channel on left current goes to wall. #27 & 28. & 29 all ran no mishaps. Ship water. #29 at Vasay's Paradise. Noon. Take moving pictures. Current divides on Island and then unites. Big waves. #30 V & big waves #31 bad rapid. I go through but break oar lock. E splashed completely. Very sheer drop big waves against wall. Channel on left. Photo of arch below Vasay's. Bridge below #30 Camp early in short box Canyon. River turns sharply South just below camp. Last day in Marble

November 14

Got up early to repair locks etc. Loaded cameras and photoed beds. Emery about ready to leave at 9.30.

We drifted or pulled down stream with new energy as we hoped to reach the Little Colo.

The walls grew much higher but wider. No rapids of any conse- Nankoweap quence up to Nancaweep Valey. We passed several side canyons where Canyon the Kiabab Plateau could be seen also land marks that were fermilliar to us.

We are eating our lunch now about 6 mi above Little Colo. We only got out once in the run to look over rapids #37 which had one large rock in center of river. It is cold but moderated after passing the Little Colo. Little

Still keeping up our good luck we reach and pass the Mormon mines Colorado and camp just below them out of sight of Grand View so they would not River see our camp signal fire as there was time for trouble and delay from here to B.A.

Next morning at Tanner ledge trouble against wall. Camp at Hances.

[*Emery's diary from here to Bright Angel Trail are missing*]

Ellsworth A long run on very swift water and a succession of one rapid after another. We divide it into 20 for the day to the mouth Little Colo. Noon opposite Nanco Weep Valley. Leave Little Colo 3 P.M. Reach Tanner Trail 4.45. Continue to a point above first sheer wall South. 12 rapids from little Colo.

November 15

Ellsworth ~~Have~~ Over one big rapid, several small. Get to Hance Trail about 10. Worst rapid yet. Conclude to portage. Carry all stuff to middle then line and portage my boat. Evening. Both very tired and sore. Emery got very close to the wall in the big rapid early in the A.M. and had rather close shave. Very large waves next to wall.

Hance
Rapid

November 16

Ellsworth I conclude to run other boat. E.C. stays near other boat and makes moving picture. Come down on the left between large rocks. Cross to middle, down channel swing to left in front of camera and land. We load boats, start at 11. In going over lower half of Hance R. Emery gets thrown out for an instant.

[*Note written in margin of page reads:* "Speed of lower part Hance Rapid 32 miles per hr."]

Sockdolager Get to Sockdologer about 12. Take a short look and conclude to run
Rapid on left or South. E keeps close to wall and ships only one inch water. I take middle and get 3 in. Fall 34½ ft in ⅓ mile. A smooth stretch then another rapid. We stop between and I leave stereo camera on rocks where we have made some pictures, including M.P.

On again over two smaller ones then another worse than Sockdologer. No rocks very rough Boats half full of water. Three miles below a big dip 14 ft high. Rust and Emery have been to this point.

Bright In next rapid Emery cuts completely through a wave, bow first, and
Angel gets a hard jolt. 8 rapids for the day. 178 ft fall. B.A. Creek at 4.30. Go up
Trail to fence and build signal fire.

Go to B.A. Trail at noon. Everet Willis and a new guide there. Walk up get home at five.

November 17
Ellsworth

Signal has been seen.
Twenty rapids above B.A. trail
Find Blanche has been sick all the time we were on trip.
Welcome home.

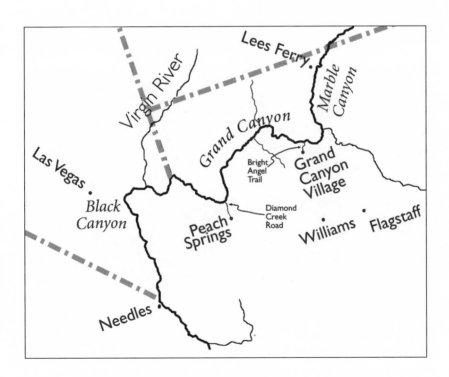

Bert Lauzon and Emery Kolb

introducing Bert Lauzon

THE KOLB BROTHERS *knew the toughest stretch of river still lay ahead, and during their one month respite on the rim began looking for someone to fill the position Jimmy Fagan had so quickly vacated. After considering several possible assistants, they finally settled on Bert Lauzon, a twenty-five year old miner and cowboy, new to the area. Like the Kolb Brothers themselves, Lauzon arrived at Grand Canyon unaware it would capture the rest of his life. Brad Cole of Cline Library, who curates the Hubert R. Lauzon Collection, offers this brief introduction:*

HUBERT "BERT" LAUZON was born in Compton Village, Quebec, Canada, on 25 January 1886, to Francois and Mary Lauzon. Francois immigrated to Colorado in the 1880s, and on 21 May 1884, became a U.S. citizen in Delta County, Colorado. According to Bert, his father homesteaded a ranch in western Colorado along the Uncompaghre River while his family still resided in Compton Village, but by the 1890s the entire family lived in Colorado.

Bert dropped out of school in 1902, and for the next two years worked cattle and trained racehorses for Verdi L. Hotchkiss of Montrose, Colorado. His interest in horses became a life long pursuit. After leaving Colorado in 1906, and before his arrival at Grand Canyon in 1911, Bert spent about four years working in mines throughout the Southwest, primarily in southern Arizona, California and northern Mexico.

Bert arrived at Grand Canyon in June 1911, and was employed as a guide and laborer by tourism operator and miner William Wallace Bass. He worked for Bass until December when he quit to become the Kolbs' assistant for the lower portion of their Colorado River trip. Bert returned to the Grand Canyon in the fall of 1913 where he remained until his death in 1951. He married Edith Bass in 1916. The couple had three children—Hubert F., Loren "Tiny", and Muriel. Tragically Edith passed away in 1923. Bert married Rosa White in 1927.

Bert worked for Coconino County as the custodian of the Bright Angel Trail from 1918 through 1928. During the same period he served as the elected Grand Canyon Precinct constable.

In 1928, Coconino County relinquished the Bright Angel Trail to the National Park Service. Bert's job as trail custodian ended, but he was hired as a park ranger, starting work on January 1, 1929. Over the next 22 years he worked as trails supervisor and as a law enforcement ranger, helped patrol park boundaries for poachers, assisted with fish plants on Clear Creek, and accompanied an expedition that investigated rumors about dwarf horses near Havasu Canyon. His long experience in Grand Canyon's backcountry working for Bass and the Kolbs and time spent as constable made him especially suited to these types of responsibilities. Hubert F. Lauzon died of silicosis on November 3, 1951, shortly following his retirement from the park service.

His son Loren "Tiny" Lauzon remembered his father as "ambitious [having] good reasoning power thought fast… no fear of anything, steady, didn't drink, good sense of humor. Magnet for people. People couldn't stay away from him."

Bradford Cole

the trip resumes

The Kolbs made the front page of the Coconino Sun *again on Friday, 24*   news item
November 1911:

KOLB BROTHERS REACH GRAND CANYON

Tired and wet, but happy, Emory C. and Ellsworth L. Kolb arrived at Grand Canyon Saturday after a 900-mile contest with the rapids of the Green and Colorado rivers during their journey from Green River, Wyoming to the gulf.

The little boat in which they made the trip was in good condition.

The Kolbs had but one upset. In Soap Creek rapids they were overturned by the rushing water and drifted down half a mile, holding to the boat before they could right it. It was the place that three members of the Brown exploring expedition lost their lives.

The Socdolager section, supposed to be the worst of the entire trip was passed in safety.

A trail guide met Emery and Ellsworth at the foot of Bright Angel Trail the next morning when they rowed across the river from Rust's Camp and advised Emery his wife was very ill. Upon reaching the studio at the rim he rushed her to Los Angeles on the next train. Blanche was pregnant and in a serious condition; had the river trip been delayed for as much as a day it could well have caused her death. From the letters left it is apparent Emery was unaware of her condition when he left Green River, Wyoming. Had he been, he no doubt would have left the trip at once and returned home.

Blanche's condition and loss of the child delayed resumption of the trip until 19 December. The Kolb brothers sent and received several important letters during this interval. One arrived from Charles Smith whom neither expected to ever hear from:

Hite Garfield Co. Utah
Nov. 15, 1911

Dear Friends

I arrived in Hite today the fifingth all O.K. I had a merry-time playing ring around some of those large boulders as i tried every posible way i could think of and a great many ways that i could not think of but anchored here at last.

The old boat is all right fore smothe water yet but wouldent stand another Canyon.

I hope your trip has been successfull and the photoes proved up all right.

Respectfully Yours
Charles F. Smith

December 12th 1911

My Dear Blanche.-

Everybody is glad to know you are coming along so fine. Ed is on the election board & E.V is now getting a litle lunch. They are cooking in the studio… The weather is simply grand and has been for some. Cold this morning but warm now… There are several fellows who want to go along and we may take some with us for help, safety, and pictures.

We have not had a chance to talk over things but I will tell you later when we expect to leave...

This is the day that tells the tale for Ralph [Cameron][16] and I am afraid it is going to be a big job for him to win.

I will not write much now as Ed has the kitchen cleaned nice so I think I will paint the floor this afternoon...

With much love to you all, I am

Truly your bunch of garlic

E.C. Kolb
Suckling of America:
O' I mean
Kipling

Dec. 12th 11

letter from Emery

Dear Wife,

Wrote you once today but before I go to bed I will chat a little more. The votes here are just counted 19 to 5 for Ralph. Too bad every presinct cannot do as well. The beautifull weather hastily diminished to give place for a flood of clouds, which after ~~giving~~ presenting a gorgeous sunset settled down on us and it is now beginning to moan and shreak, then a hush came over us like the hush of death. What does it mean? Why the whole mountain is soon to be enveloped in a snowy garb, covering the few blades of grass, flowers and the wood pile. Inside the ranch house is a slow fire, the click of the small clock sounds like a sledge and the paint from the floor gives up an odor like the dead, "Nuf said."...

One of the fellows just dropped in to see if we wanted him for the trip. We may start with two.

Business is not very brisk yet but travel is picking up.

Now the sleet is pounding at the door...

I may give the floor another coat of paint tomorrow then again I may not.

Ed had everything all cleaned up, he brought up some cooking utincils from the canyon to cook with and is getting a supply of stuff from Montgum Ward & Co. He has been dealing with Babbitts.

Well good night dear I hope you will rest well tonight. We will likely not start before Monday...

From you loving husband
Emery

Dec. 18 1911

My Dearest Wife.

This morning I regestered you some money, hope you get it ok. Yes I think I have been getting all of your letters, and they are a comfort to me. I don't know anytime in our life that I longed to be with you as I have since coming back. I guess it is because everything is in such a confusion that I am nervous and nead your petting. I guess when we get started I can through some of this lonesomness off. It is genuine winter and ½ ft. of snow. The snow went clear down to the gardens. We sent Earnest & our man down with a load to the boats this evening and Ed & ~~we~~ I expect to get a man & mule from El Tovar to pack the rest of our goods in the morning. Bass[17] is going to take provisions for us down his trail and Earnest will come out there... Miss Moran was all ready to go down and see us leave this morning but we were not ready then beside it was snowing very hard. It is still snowing but we will likely leave in the morning anyway just so as to get our start then the balance comes easier...

Well girlie I don't know what else to tell you at present but shall hold this until morning so to let you know if we leave or not.

After we eat our cake I may write more.

Well we had our bite and I just took a bath and have attired myself in red.

The snow keeps falling but we have ordered our mule for 7-30 am... I feel better this eve since we have things straightened up and if we get started in the morning we will be happy. This is all for tonight dear and I'll leave this little space below for morning to let you know if we get off.

Good night girlie

"Good Morning"

As this morning is clear I guess we are now off for sure, so good by sweetheart and don't worry for we will soon be togather again...

Your affectionate Emery

The youngest brother, Ernest ("E.V.") was to accompany Emery and Ellsworth down the river to the foot of Bass Trail where he would return to the studio to attend to what little business there was until Blanche was able to be at the Grand Canyon again. The brothers descended the Bright Angel Trail on 18 December through six inches of fresh snow. During their month on the rim, the Colorado River had dropped four feet.

After considering several new assistants, the Kolbs hired a young man named Hubert R. Lauzon to accompany them all the way to Needles, California.

December 17
Bert

Maurice [*Bert's brother*] came up to Grand Canyon at 8 A.M. I met him at the train and went around with him. Was snowing hard, first big snow of the winter. Bass went to Grandview with two young ladies.

December 18
Bert

We were down at the studio in the morning getting ready to start down. After dinner. Ernest (Kolb) and I packed a horse and started down Bright Angel Trail. About a foot of snow on the rim and a couple of inches at the Indian Gardens, raining at the River. Ernest took the horse up to the half way house and stayed all night, I rolled my bed down in the sand for the night.

December 19
Emery

Departed from End of B.A. trail 2 P.M. Evert witnessed our start making a couple pictures. Also saw people watching from the plateau as we passed. Saw but one person as we ran the large rapid visable from plateau.

Camped in side canyon just opposite dead man below figure 7. 4 Pm.

Ellsworth

Remain at home until Dec. 19.

Snow on top

~~Emery~~ Ernest Kolb & Bert Lauzon packed Jess [*name of mule?*] and went to boats yesterday. We got a guide Evert Willis and a pack mule and sent him ahead. We follow getting there at 12 Don't eat, get started at 2. Rather a bad whirl pool for a little rapid in second part. I dip a little water. We reach Pyrites rapid at 3. Parties on plateau watch us run rapid. We camp less than a mile below on north side nice wide sand in side canyon.

Horn
Creek
Rapid

Bert **Ed (Ellsworth) and Emery got down to the river at 10:00 AM. We left the trail at 2:00 PM, ran two rapids and made camp only a few miles from the trail. There was a skeleton of a man up on the rocks across the river from us.**

December 20

Emery After breakfast two of us climbed up the granite ~~where~~ to see if we could find location of skeleton which we covered up with rocks in 1906, but finding it to be some distance higher returned to boats.

We were soon to the Salt Creek rapid and after manuvering around for about an hour we ran both boats through while Earnest took some snap 5x7 of us and Bert a moving pictures. The waves were heavy and both our cockpits were filled to the seat making boats fairly uncontrollable.

I landed at the foot of rapid but Ed was unable to do the same and had to run a long stretch of swift water before he could land. Earnest & I climbed a small cliff and could not see Ed below.

As soon as Bert had *Edith* bailed I followed down with both he and Earnest and found Ed unharmed bailing out. We continued on and

Granite Falls about an hour later was figuring how to run the Monument Creek rapid. The one seen from Hopi Point. It was quite a long one and had two large submerged rocks which the currant ran again. Earnest took a moving P of E & I running the rapid and said we were out of sight frequently. Bert stayed near the foot of the rapid with a rope in case of accident also to make 5x7 snap of us. We landed and ate lunch at the foot of the rapid.

Hermit Rapid Next came a rapid where we concluded was Hermit Stream on South, I hit a rock and got into big waves. Our next rapid was a very long one & full of rocks, much resembling the rapids of the upper canyons. A stream came in from the north which we concluded was Crystal Creek. After striking many rocks we landed at the bottom and took Earnest and Bert on again. We had not traveled long until we came to another rapid but as it was near dark we camped on the north.

Ellsworth **Cold & cloudy. Sun comes out a few times Start at 9.**

Take boys over couple small rapids get to Salt Creek Rapid at about 10. Get 5x7 and M.P. Camera out and let the boys take pictures as we

run her. Rather rough and we do not go through in channel we pick out but are carried through big waves near shore. I ship so much water I cannot make landing above little rapid but go over it and another E lands and gets boys on. Bail out Reach Monument Creek at 12. Spend an hour getting cameras ready. Very rough lots of rocks. We pick channel on left or South. E goes first. We both go over big rock I scrape and we both fill up considerably. Noon. My boat leaks badly. ~~Thurs Dec 2 Later find last rapid is Hermit not Monument~~ Come to Rapid at Louis trail. Very rocky. Pick channel on South then swing to center. Both run it successfully but touch a few rocks.

Camp at Crystal Creek that night

Broke camp at 8 AM. The boys ran Salt and Monument Creek and Hermit Rapids. Hermit Creek rapids were long and rough. We got moving and still pictures of them. This is where Russell and Monette are supposed to have lined on the North side but that is impossible as the north wall is sheer to the waters edge. Bert

December 21

Seeing it would be difficult ~~to ha~~ for the boys to climb around the rapid we were about to run; we decided to take both of them through with us. This we did and with success. Emery

The next rapid was divided into 4 divisions three of these we ran, then landed at the head of the 4th. making a moving picture of our signals and running the *Edith* down past a large granite rock which had fallen into the middle of the river. We came onto a small rapid apparently smoothe water rushing under the S. wall; this did not look bad so we started through with out examination. Earnest with E's boat and Bert ~~with~~ in mine. *Defiance* took the lead & when near the foot we saw her tied up on a rock as it appeared to us. We shot by them close to the wall and pulled into a whirl below. Earnest was laying on his stomach clinging to the boat and was being douced with heavy waves quite frequently. Ells. oars were loose and held down by the currant so he was helpless. We could not imagine what held her there and knew by the way she was being thrown that something would soon happen. The cockpit filled and then with another lounge she turned over with Earnest & Ed under her. It was done so quick neither of them held to the boat and both were out of sight several seconds. Ear. came up first 20 ft. below the boat swimming tward the wall. We pulled for him, Bert tossing a rope which Ear. caught. B scrambled on the stern reaching for Ear, while I held ~~his~~ B by the heel. we pulled Ear in the boat and saw Ed holding onto the upset boat. She looked as though he would be chrushed again the wall but she swung out and we pulled for her. Ed was now on top and we soon were all 4 in *Edith*. We landed on the North and soon had all our goods drying. Our M.P. camera in water film wet cameras wet everything wet. After drying out the worst of things we packed up as we did not want to camp by the rapid where we were upset. Followed down, ran 1 with B & Ev. in. Then came to a very heavy rapid with sheer walls, so had to run with B & E. on board. We went through successfully but after passing the heavy water both boats were carried again the S wall and a hole several inches long was put in a plank on *Edith*.

We stuck a glove in the hole and continued on to the head of a small rapid. Then camped.

Ellsworth **Big rapid just below camp. Ran it successfully. Still water then three rather swift ones close together called one rapid. Put the boys on shore and run it. Below large rock blocks channel, swift water. Take boys on board and run past it.**

Just below current goes over one rock and against wall I miss channel go over rock and boat is held by water pouring in from all sides: finally upsets Ernest loses hold on boat I hang on. Boys take him in. I climb on top of boat. Land and dry out. Ran two more big rapids after upset. Camp.

Bert **Ran 5 rapids today, 11 up to date. Ed got into a dip on the lower side of a rock and stuck there for awhile, finally the boat tipped over and Ernest came down in the ice cold river at 20 miles an hour and Ed following on top of the upturned boat. Emery and I had made it thru all right and as Ernest was shooting into the wall I caught him by a handkerchief he had tied around his neck and pulled him into our boat also got Eds boat and made a landing on the north side of the river. Photographic stuff all wet, made a fire and some hot toddies and got dinner, pulled out about 3 PM. While running a** rapid just before dark we hit the wall, broke a hole in the side of the boat, we stuffed a pair of gloves in the hole and ran the rest of the rapid and camped for the night.

December 22
Emery
Bass
Trail

Ran both boats thru 1s small rapid then ran 5 big ones and one just above Bass cable.

Ellsworth

Run six rapids taking the boys over two of them. One is very big drop with sheer walls on either side, make it safely. Reach Bass cage 1.30 camp for noon under cage. Find John, Berts brother Morris, and Cecil Dodd. Ernest goes up trail with John. John returns in the evening after getting a horse for Ernest.

Bert

We ran and got pictures of several rapids. Scared up an otter and got to Bass Ferry at 1:30 PM. Maurice, John [Waltenberg][18] and Cecil [Dodd] were at the ferry when we got there. Got dinner and dried out our clothing. Maurice and Cecil went to the Shinumo for a cooking outfit. Ernest took a camera and exposed plates and went to the rim with John. 4th camp.

Dec 22nd. 11
Bass Cable

letter from
Emery

Dear Blanche;

As usual we are a day or so late. Just landed here a 2 P.M. We are sending this out with Earnest.

There are 3 men here, old John and a brother of the fellow who is with us.

We are all in good order but in an upset lost all pictures we had made on our way. We saved the M.P. camera but it is not all together dried out yet. We ran some pretty bad rapids some had to take the boys through with us as the walls were sheer.

I poked a hole in my boat but had it fixed in a jiffy this morning and we ran 6 big fellows this morning.

We saw a pretty otter this morn.

Now dear I would write you a big letter but we must send Earnest up right away. I want you to be good patient now and dont worry even if we don't get out as soon as we planed. I send you much love, also to Edith,

I don't know for sure that we will come out at Peach Springs as we are not certain just where diamond Creek is.

The man we have now is just fine, he takes right hold and is good all round fellow.

Glad to have the chance of sending this out to you as it will probably be the last for some time.

Dinner is now called so good by.

Give my regards to the folks

Your loving husband.

Emery

December 23

Emery   Repair M.P. Camera. Take pictures of old John in drama of stealing boats.

Ellsworth   **Clear and Cold.**

The boys help us take some moving pictures as John has gone for tools. Do not move camp.

Bert   **Took some MPs of John and Maurice as they crossed on the cage. John went over to the Copper. Worked up a Drama with Maurice as the Sheriff, Cecil as Outlaw, stealing Emerys boat.**

Emery wrote a letter to Ernest on a page torn from his journal book:

letter from
Emery

Bass Cable

Dec. 24th, 11

Dear Brother.

We did not get away the next day and here it is 1 PM today and just leaving. We found some trouble with our camera beside drying everthing out. I hope you did not suffer with the cold the night you went up, and that you got into the house OK.

We made several rolls film which we are sending you from here. Please put it with the other up in the house and be very carefull of it. We will likely send for it from Needles to be shipped to Calif.

We have powder for fish so will have a Xmas here tomorrow. Eh.

We worked up a drama of boat steeling here. Old John figures in it.

Ed and I are going to leave soon we finished the play at Shiniumo rapid which Ed has run & I will now Take Bert and give him the necessary baptism.

Mail this to Blanche.

E & I wish you a merry Xmas ducking.

Enclosed with the letter was a note to his wife:

Dear Blanche

You can see by this we are not making the best headway but the pictures we have got here will go out dry. Tomorrow is Xmas and I hope you have a good time.

We are just now giving a meal for the three actors and we three.

Love and best wishes to you all

From your own

  hubby

  Emery

Dear Blanche-Bass just brought this in this eve.

letter from Emery

Finish our drama at the head of Shimumo Creek rapid. Have dinner for all six. Leave John & the boys about 2 P.M. running Bert over the Shin. rapid. The descent of the river is very rapid and while the rapids are not bad the water is uncontrolable.

December 24
Emery
Shinumo Rapid
110-Mile Rapid

We ran No 2 in 4 sections and at the end of this series it dropped abruptly amoung large boulders but we ran it safely. No. 3 was easy, then we had a fine stretch from the asbestoes until a side canyon formed an ugly rapid. We sent Bert below. Ed led and was hurled out of his course all most instantly and being carried for the big drop below. Seeing this I put extra effort to the N. side and got mixed in a nest of rocks which held my boat. I watched Ed as he dissapeared over the dip. He did not pass but was held by the recoil waters. In another instant the boat went over and still held by the waters but Ed did not come up for quite a while. When he did he was about 50 ft below the boat which also floated out and righted itself. The rapid was long and I had fear

Hakatai Rapid
Walthenberg Rapid

that Ed may drown as the water being ice cold and freezing some along the edges of the river.

I strained every muscle to get my boat off the rocks which I finaly did and pulled for the ~~deep water~~ big waves though I knew it may mean my life, but Ed was fast going toward another rapid.

I went over dip, hit rock smashed side of boat and filled to the gunwales.

Ed's boat got in a whirlpool and Bert swam out and rowed her in. I landed on the N. side just above Ed who just crawled out in time. We were landed on a bunch of rocks with hardly room to stand. Though inexperienced our nervy Bert rowed Ed's boat over to us. Ed could hardly speak but said I want to shake your hand. There was but little wood but we soon had dry clothes out and some hot drink. Ed's narrow escape from drowning kept him awake.

Ice hung on the rocks.

Ellsworth **We finish the picture at noon lunch at head of Bass rapid after I have run boat through. Emery finishes a moving picture film on the rapid then we pack and send all exposed film out with John. Next rapid is divided into several smaller ones with a very rocky one at bottom. Pass it safely on South. Large rocks in center. #3. Big waves clear channel in center swift water all the time. #4 is full of bad rocks all over. I go first, go over big rock and the water churning in from all sides holds me there. I see Emery is hung up on rock at head of rapid. My boat is filled and thrown from side to side finally turns over with me under. I lose hold on gunwale as the boat is turned completely over** [*What appears to be a caret (^) follows and the words* "right side up" *are written at the top of the page.*] **Long time under water in the swift current. Come up only to be carried under time and again by the big waves. Waves finally dwindle. I see Bert running opposite on shore (South) boat near him. I try to go that way but current takes me across. Have rubber coat on, high boots, two preservers. Almost exhausted. More choppy waves then I get to side in still water and just manage to paddle to shore (North shore) before going over another rapid. Bert swims out and catches boat in whirlpool. I can hardly drag myself out. Motion to Bert asking for Emery. E climbs on rock above me and says his boat** is smashed. Bert crosses my boat to where I am at a little ~~hole~~ cove in rocks Emery brings his boat down. Smashed in center on right side about two feet. All four boards broken two ribs. Camp. [*Words written in right hand margin* "5 minutes later clothes frozen."]

Bert

Finished the drama with John as prospector. Ate lunch with the crowd and pulled out for Needles at 2:30. Ran 3 rapids and came to a bad one at 4 PM. I went to the lower end with a long rope to throw out if the boys were upset and came my way. Ed went over a big dip and was swept down the River for 1500 ft. Just got out at the head of another rapid in time. He was all in and nearly froze. Emery was hung up on a rock at the head of rapid, got loose, went over a big rock hit another rock just below and smashed the central compartment of his boat. Ed's boat hung up in a whirlpool on my side of the river 100 ft. out. Most of our grub and repair outfit was in this boat. I had to swim for it—got the boat—baled it out with my hat and crossed to where Ed was. About this time Emery came in with the crippled boat. After we got a fire and dry clothes on and a good supper we felt good and lucky that we were all together. Camped on a big pile of boulders.

December 25
Emery

We [were] very happy to be all together & alive. It took me the whole day to repair the hole in my boat. Large enough to crawl through. Carried beds through rocks to sand bar.

Took pictures.

Christmas at Walthenberg Rapid

Ellsworth **Xmas**

Emery works all day on boat puts in ribs uses bottom of floor planking for pieces. Makes a fine job. Take a few pictures of repair, rapid, etc. No plates or film lost. Cold.

Bert Xmas morn were all stiff and cold from the day before, got breakfast rustled wood across the river, made a mesquite rib and got the boat repaired. Took some MP and photos of smashed boat, painted a (Merry Xmas) sign and got a picture of the camp.

December 26

Emery Left camp late and ran a rapid at once. Very swift water and then a fine quiet stretch. We ran 5 rapids and some riffles. Ran out of the granite. Scenery much like lower marble canyon. Beautifull camp, fine weather but cold.

Ellsworth Finish job on E's boat with canvass white lead and tin. Start at 11. Run 2 rapids and a great deal of swift water, get out of granite. Turn ~~north~~ east then south. Noon. Turn north again beautiful scenery in marble walls ~~again~~. A lot of little rapids ~~and~~ swift water and two big rapids. Five rapids for the day. Camp at turn of river near point opposite Lee's Canyon on top. Top is snow covered. Beautiful valley ~~like formation~~ at river. Camp on right.

Bert Left Xmas rapids at 11 AM. Got out of the first granite section after 5 miles of good swift water and no rocks, fine going in sandstone. rough going. Made 10 miles in the sandstone and camped. Saw the bottom of a big boat hung up on a big boulder in the middle of the river. Ran 5 rapids.

December 27

Emery The past night was a bad one for me. Heavy cold settled in my throat. I took chill so called Ed who got up and put some water on to heat. A bruised and frost bitten toe gave me much pain I soaked it in hot water then lineament and after having a hot drink went to bed and slept. We left camp about 10 am and soon ran 5 rapids. The granite now appeared again with a sand strata laying on top the uplifted granite.

The 3rd. rapid in the granite had two dips similar to those Ed had 2 upsets, but we decide to run it. I lead and find myself too weak to keep out the dip. Was carried in sidewise and the boat turned throwing me into the water. I clung to an oar which was tied. In another second I climbed on top the upset boat reached down and found an oar. With this I paddeled to shore on top the upset boat. Bert threw a rope as I neared and we soon had our photo goods out drying. I changed my clothes and in 2 hours we were on our way. Lunched here before starting. (icy) We next came to a rapid with an island of granite in the river. **Bedrock Rapid** The main body of water went thru a space not more than 30 ft wide. no telling how deep. Ed ran both boats thru on the N. side. One more and then a heavy one where we are now camped and have *Edith* lined ½ way **Deubendorff Rapid** down the rapid. Out of the granite again. Pass 2 small streams 1 little fall to N.W.

My B̶ birthday.   **Ellsworth**

Ran 10 rapids 5 in the sandstone or lime 5 in the second granite No. 8 for the day had two curling waves. very heavy bad approach. Emery got caught in first turned over climbed on top of boat and steered to shore. Bert threw rope to him. I followed safely. Two hours spent drying photo supplies and Lunch. Camp early beside a heavy rapid. Dry canyon on right for camp. Line Emery's boat half way down. Moonlight, clear and very cold. Freezing all day. Rapid #9 has a granite Island in center. Channel on East or right. Take a photo at No. 10

Running Bedrock Rapid, going right of the island

showing end of granite. Algonkin shows, looking North White strata possibly serpentine 400 ft. above river.

Bert Ran 5 miles and 5 rapids in sandstone and entered a narrow granite gorge which we went through in 5 miles. Emense high walls and narrow river. Sandstone section about 10 miles long. Emery was tipped over in the rapid in the granite and got on top of the upturned boat before the water got thru his slicker. I threw a rope to him and pulled him to shore. 37 rapids up to date. Camped at the head of a bad rapid, asbestos formation showing up above our camp. Trocolite sandstone and serpentine. Just leaving Powell Plateau.

December 28

Emery Line *Defiance* down to where *Edith* was and loaded. Ran lower half of rapid. one more rapid then came to Tapeach creek. Rapid quite bad. Ed

Tapeats Creek ran both boats also ran both boats at No 4 and No. 5 beginning granite. Rapid ran to S. wall but we get thru after hard work.

Deer Creek Falls 2 mile granite quite as pond. at lower end came beautifull surprise fall about 100 ft. high. As we were viewing it we discovered a handsome bighorn sheep gazing upon us. [*The words* "(cliff dwellings)" *written in between the lines.*] He got away before our camera was on him. The last rapid of the day was a side canyon from the North. quite bad 2 dips and *Edith* nearly upset getting in sideways.

We pitched our darkroom and slept in it as it rained. The snow nearly reached down to us. Ice covered all boulders near shore.

Ellsworth Run 10 rapids. Line the one at camp. Reach Tapeats Creek about 1½ mile below camp. about the size of B. A. or larger. Rather a bad rapid #2 for the day. Run it on left. Take pictures with graflex. #5 lies at head of 3rd granite which is about 2 miles long no rapids in it. Come to surprise falls at end. See Mt. Sheep. He runs away. Falls about 200 ft high ft high in the open then cork screws in a narrow slot.

This section is full of wonderful formation, uplifts intrusions etc. The serpentine runs about 3 miles on top of troculite 100 ft above the river, found on both sides. At #9 the blue lime wall comes down close to River on South. Other side lifted high. Most of these rapids swing against wall on turns and have a shoal on other side. Rather difficult to approach. #10 rapid has two large curlers half way down. Emery goes first, wind turns him sideways and he almost turns over but doesn't. I follow stern first give a hard shove and clear. Camp here at mouth of narrow Canyon. Driftwood 75 ft above River. Clouding up and looks stormy.

We line the two boats over bad rapid at camp this morning. Got into the ice water up to my neck. Trocolite that the river runs in. A strata of serpentine capped by lime extends down both sides of the river for about 3 miles. We got to Tapech Creek before lunch. Below Tapech is an uplift where the Algonkians show for a mile or so. Below, the river follows a fault that shows lots of iron in the schist. The north side is broken all to pieces, a formation shows there that looks like tufa but is green shale I believe. 10 rapids for the day, rode them all. Made about 8 miles. Have been in Sandstone for about 3 miles. The Plateau has tapered until now the walls are sheer to the top of the blue lime. Have traveled 58 or 60 miles so far. At 3 PM we came to a beautiful waterfall coming in from the north side with a fall of about 100 ft. At this place we saw a big Mt. Sheep which was a dandy. Ed tried to get a picture with his graflex but the camera stuck on him and the sheep started off. I put in a couple of shots with a six shooter but did not hit him. *Bert*

December 29

Cold & raining snow above. We get up late. As the boys busy themselves I take M.P. Camera apart and have success repairing it. We have just lunched and it is now snowing while I write. After the sky cleared we hurried things together and drifted down a swift current and in an hour found us at the mouth of Kanab Creek. Walls of lime grew high and sheer. Mt. Sheep tracks every where. *Emery*

Kanab Creek

Think we hear a shot but see no one though at creek were old foot prints of a man. Take pictures and run a long rapid swift water and another rapid. Camp on S. bank by little stream.

Ran 2 rapids. Camped 3 miles below Kanab. Only ran two hours today Rained all night and all morning by spells. Snow came within 300 ft of River. Clouds hanging low. We had the dark room up last night and it helped keep our cameras and stuff dry also E. C. and I. Bert was covered with his tarp. E.C. fixed up the M.P. Camera which was *Ellsworth* giving us trouble. I took some views and changed oars. After dinner rained again. Made a one hour run to Kanab Creek. Stopped and made photos. See old foot prints. A long easy rapid below the Creek. Run it, swift water below, then another rapid. Some large waves but no trouble. Camp by a little stream on left. We put up dark room loaded M.P. Camera and 8x10's and took room down again. Have everything put away for more rain as it looks stormy. Bert has made 3 flap jacks. Firewood scarce & wet.

Bert   Snowed and rained last night, wood was all wet, lots of trouble to start a fire. Snow line came nearly to the River. Took some pictures up and down the River Scenery is magnificent, walls straight up and nearly a mile high. Emery fixed the lens of the Moving Picture camera. Ate lunch and pulled down the River to Kanab Canyon—about 4 miles. Kanab is where Powell left the River in 1871 for Utah abandoned the trip on account of high water. Made some pictures of the mouth of Canyon which is a regular box. Nice stream of water coming in. About 90 miles to Kanab. Ran two rapids and camped 4 miles from Kanab. The walls are sheer to the Carboniferous. Pass some formation that looks like green shale in the Sandstone.

December 30

Emery   Prepair for early start but hang up several hours to fix M.P. Camera. Walls sheer and a good current. Set dark room up to fix M.P. camera at 1st rapid n.g. [?] Next rapid quite long. Bad take off. One large boulder Upset Rapid   in center of river another dip below it. Either would upset our boats. Pack most our goods below rapid and make fire for lunch. Ed does not feel like running it but I feel confident. I go first and make good but bump a few submerged rocks in the take off.

     We continue on a very swift river, fairly dropping in front of us.

     The walls still seem higher and the river is not more than 50 ft. wide in places. We run another rapid. Big water. The last for the day and 4th was a sudden dip as boulders fairly blocked the river. We made it easily and continued on a beautifull smooth stretch of water for about 2 Havasu Creek   mi. The walls looked fermilliar so we knew we were near Cateract. Bad landing. Pull boats accross Cat.

     Wood scarce. Camp on rocks beside Creek.

Camp at Cataract Canyon. Ran 4 rapids to-day lots of swift riffles and good water for boating. Lost 3 to 4 hrs. repairing M.P. Camera and taking pictures Some of the greatest and most impressive walls we have seen yet. Nothing grander than the mouth of Cataract however, which we have seen twice before. 1st rapid easy, nothing but water. 2nd looks bad. Shoal at start on right and bad channel ending with bad suck holes below rocks. The only channel is on right shore to close to a bad whirl or comber. We carry most of our load below rapid which enables us get over the shoal although we scrape many rocks. We both make the channel by hard work. #4 is formed by a lot of rock daming the river. A very narrow channel twists between two of these rocks. We both make it safely. Very cold all day.

The boys catch two fish. Cold clear and moonlight tonight.

On the back of the page of the journal for this date Ellsworth has written the names and address of people he has met along the way:

Mrs. Robt. Johnston
Vernal Utah.
2 ladies at Alhandra Ferry. Fruit. Send photos.
A. M. Steele,
Buell Dam
P.O. Green River Utah.
T.F. Degeurnette
Bridge Port, Utah
F.D. Watson
Lee's Ferry, Ariz.
Foreman Dredge.
L.D. Cochran
Lee's Ferry, Ariz.
B. A. Neider
Lee's Ferry, Ariz.
Send samples of pictures taking at Lee's.

Broke camp early, freezing cold, ran 4 rapids, total of 50 to date. Ed and Emery got some good pictures. shot for fish and got 3 bony-tails. Not much

Matkatamiba Rapid

change in the canyons looks. One bad rapid we unloaded the boats and carried the load to other end of rapid and they came through in good shape. This rapid had a big rapid in center and one on each side lower down. We made Cararact just at dark. Had some trouble making landing and getting wood.

December 31

Emery   Left Cateract about 10 A.M. Weather very cold. Water would freeze on clothes as soon an it splashed us. Ran rapid at Cat. Ed hit rock. #2 quite easy. Nooned at #3 & made M.P. picture of signaling. Currint bad again S. Wall. Caught some fish. ran another rapid and Camped on S. bank. E. & I shaved. Find a room of rock where we sleep. Very fine camp. During the day we made some 8 x10's. Walls about the highest we have seen. Snow capped peaks occaisonally.

Ellsworth   [*Written across the top of the page are the words* "Note. Cataract Canyon here means Havasupai."]

    Broke camp at 11 A.M. Took a number of photos at mouth of Cataract and vicinity. Camped early in the P.M. opposite a Canyon coming in from the N.W. Run for a day possibly 14 miles. Four rapids. #3 rather a rough one, with big dips over rocks. Put up M.P. Camera and worked out a film on signaling above rapid, etc. Run rapid safely but it was a little exciting at times. The boys go fishing. Get 16 bony tails. Most of them small.

Perfect camp under a shelving rock, with the side blocked by the rock which has fallen out leaving a sort of tunnel. Lots of driftwood and we hang dark room at one end and have a nice bedroom. Walls at this point are even higher than Cataract. Snow on top. Just above where we are camped is a 2 mile aisle straight away with symetrical sides, blocked by the turn at either end. Happy New Years.

Left Cataract at 10 AM, ran three rapids before lunch, fished and got 18 bony-tails, Ran 1 rapid after lunch. Canyon walls straight up from the River. Made camp under a rim rock in a natural cave enclosed on 3 sides, a most beautiful camp. I cooked a fine fish supper which we all enjoyed emensly.   Bert

Notes Suprise falls comes in above Kanab about 4 miles. We saw footprints of a man in the sand at this place, also passed some cliff dwellings on the side of the river under a ledge of rocks. Tracks were probably 10 days old. We also thought we heard a shot at this place and answered but got no reply.

Morning not so cold. Got an early start. Lime walls grow higher. Many stretches making perfect aisles for a straight mile. Catch some fish. Noon in sunlite for a change. Ran 5 medium sized rapids. Ed hit some rocks. Large block of lava sticks up in river. Take small photos. Lava has poured over the N. wall of lime some places resting on conglomerate. Only thin layer at first as lime wall shows through in places. A mile further down it has dammed the river.   January 1 1912   Emery

We camped at lava falls and lined our boats over it. Take M.P. but very dark. Ice on rocks make work difficult but we get both boats over in two hours. We are tired. Ed fell in the water several times.   Lava Falls

~~Run 4 rapids for the day. #1 rather long, medium below cataract. #8 is rough considerable drop and rocky and swings against wall.~~   Ellsworth

Ran 5 medium sized rapids, lots of swift water and camped at Lava Falls portaging our boats over the later. Caught a few fish at noon. Walls continue similar to Cat. C. or even higher till we get 2 miles from

Lava Falls then Lava breaks in. One round formation sticking out of river 35 ft high 30 ft in diamater. Falls are 12 or 14 ft high very rough.

Bert   Left Camp 15 miles down the river from Cataract, we have traveled about 100 miles so far. Opposite camp a canyon came in with some running water, there were 4 monuments [*mining claim cairns*] at the mouth of this canyon but no notices. Ran 5 rapids, passed some big cinder cones that stood up in the middle of the river and got to the famous Lava Falls at 4 PM. Lined and portaged these falls in 1 hour and 20 minutes. There was no channel here, big boulders clear across. We are all wet to the neck. There are some large hot springs on the south side of the river at this place. The steam rising from these springs looked like smoke from a campfire before we got down to them. There are some fine little falls coming out of these springs. Saw a mans tracks in the sand again today on the north side of the river. Passed two canyons coming in from the north side today. Right here is the first lava flow coming in from Mt. Trumbull.

Springs below Lava Falls

Carry our loads down and place in boats. Make a little M.P. picture of
hot springs just below falls. Cannot find dikes as per letter. 10 mile to
Toroweap. Camp 5 or 6 mile below Toro.

Granite appears for a short distance. Run 4 rapids, one a mile long,
none bad swift water all day.

*[The word "**mistake**" written at the top of page.]*

~~Cold night Jan.2.12 Tuesday.~~ Carry our loads below rapid. Take pictures of hot springs lava etc. Run 10 miles to Toroweap camp 5 miles
below on left. Granite comes out one mile below Tor. then goes back
again. One rapid below Lava one mile long broken very swift water all
day. No big rapids

Divide it into four rapids.

Left Lava Falls at 10 AM. Big change in general looks of canyon today. Could
get to the top nearly anywhere from River. Just below Lava Falls is where
Dellenbaugh came in from the north side 40 years ago. Powells map shows
walls 2000 feet straight up but it is not so. Ate lunch 1 mile above where
Torro Weap valley comes in from the north, big lava flows into the River
from the North side that damed the river 6 or 7 hundred ft., also looks if
Lava came in from the south. These flows have changed the course of the
river from one side of the canyon to the other. Ran 4 rapids and lots of swift
water. Willows and cottonwood trees growing on the banks.

Counted 4 rapids, lined 1 but all day continued in short small rapids we
did not count. Granite appears again for short distance.

Ran a bad rapid here. Below this rapid find a fault. Sedimentary on
one side, granite on the other.

Lava had run over the Sed. At 3 P.M. we come to a short rapid, the
most like a dam we have seen.

It is certainly a bad one and we dicide to line it as rocks are scattered
all thru it. Easy to line. All work done in an hour & 20 min. Run on
swift water for about an hour longer. Pass a yellow formation which
looks like a pumpkin. Camp at dark on N. side.

Full moon. Weather moderates.

Lauzon ready to rescue

Ellsworth   Broke camp at 9 : A.M. Ran 4 rapids. lined 1. #3 near point where Canyon turns S.W. below a little outcrop of granite. Falls about 12 ft, rough & rocky. We make it O.K.

Below this there is a fault with granite on left sedimentary on right. Fault turns off in side canyon. We noon here. About 3 P.M. we come to a very bad rapid possibly 15 ft. fall more of a sheer fall than anything we have seen yet. Full of rocks every where and not water enough to cover them. It is very short and we are lined past it and ready to go on in 1 hr 20 min. Granite keeps cropping out and dissapearing ~~at differ-~~ ~~ent places~~. We camp on right or West. ~~Full moon~~. An hour before we camp we pass a peculiar formation caused by the sediment of a mineral spring some what like Yellowstone. Color yellow as gold about 15 ft long. Full moon.

Hokie Pog Canyon somewhere near Toroweap on South side is Old Indian Crossing. Muddy Wittickie 15 miles below Diamond Creek Bad rapid.

Got an early start and ran 5 rapids and a small bad one before lunch. Lava flows still in canyon after 2 days of running or 40 miles. Got to a bunch of Granite at 3 PM also the nearest thing to a waterfall that I have seen on the river to date. Drops all in a bunch lined both boats in 1 hour 20 minutes. The walls are going higher than they were yesterday. Expect to make diamond creek tomorrow. A full moon and a beautiful night.   Bert

January 4

Had a nice night for sleeping. The weather is warmer though still freez-   Emery
ing.

Ran 7 rapids. The 1st bad one made M.P. picture. Ed ran both boats. Large curler in center. Kind that upset a boat easily. Runs his past easily. *Edith* nearly got smothered but got on top finnaly and came through. Ran many small ones we did not count.

Many smoothe stretches of water. About noon I see smoke down the river. We were sure this time it was not a warm spring as before. Land at head of heavy water rapid. Call but get no reply. Go up & find an old man cooking some baken. He was about 70. J. P. Schnider. We had heard of him up in Ladore Canyon and is a half brother to Chatwin the Jenson P.M.

He said Diamond creek was 2 mile below. Took a couple of snaps him. He was very accomidaten. Also got in M.P. picture while we ran the rapid.

Smoothe water 2 mile or more brought us to Diamond. Nice little   Diamond
stream. We lunch. Get out films to take to Peach Springs. We are out   Creek
of flour. Ed ran *Edith* over long rapid below with all beds in her. Left *Defiance* above till morning. B & I walk or climb along sides down to the foot. I carrying M.P. camera with strap over shoulder. Fell and I'm nearly thrown into river from above by the weight of camera pulling me. Camp on N. side. Clouding up.

Ran 7 rapids for the day. #3 rather a rough one. Made a moving and   Ellsworth
graflex photo of running both boats. #6 big water. At this point we see a camp fire and on investigating find an old prospector John P Snyder, a half brother of Chatrin, ~~Jenson Chatrin~~ the Jensen Post Master in a little dug out. He gives us much information and appears glad to see us. We get him in a M.P.

#7 is the long rapid below Diamond Creek. We camp at the bottom. An easy rapid with 16 ft. fall.

Bert **Ran 7 rapids shortly after leaving camp. Passed some good-looking country for mineral. Big iron dikes on south side of River. Got to third granite at 9:30 AM. Got some moving pictures of third rapid. Came on to an old gent named J.P. Schyneder camped in a canyon two miles above Diamond Creek. The boys took some pictures of Schyneder. He knew trappers way up in the head waters of the Green. Was doing some placering there. Ran 7 rapids—78 to date. Got some moving pictures of the boy[s] running rapid a with Schyneder on the bank watching them. Schyneder told us of an experience he and his brother had while crossing above the rapid on a raft with his brother. They went over the rapid and 4 miles down the river yesterday we passed a mineral spring that was the color and shape of a big squash. Ran the Diamond creek rapid and camped below on north side of river.**

January 5

Emery Get up at 5.30 and prepare for long walk to Peach Springs. Ed runs *Defiance* down and we all cross. Leave river 9.10 AM. About 1 mile up Diamond is an old house where Farley used to keep tourists. The right hand canyon from there we gradually pick our way each carrying about 20 lbs.

Vegetation differs showing a warmer climate. Many ocateas, black chaprell (spines) Palaverde with its drooping clusters, and many cactus.

We eat lunch on our way up. spring half way out. Get to pump house about 4 P.M. 5 mi. from Peach Springs very cold, Snow. Got to P.S. after

Peach Springs Arizona dark. Have hard time getting supper. Do so finaly from pumpers wife, also breakfast. Nelsons fix us up with a bed. Send telegrams. ~~next day Exp. films~~ etc.

Ellsworth **We leave camp at 9 A.M. and pack our exposed & surplus film & plates out to Peach Springs. ~~Diamond Creek~~ 25 miles distant. Meals at pumpers home, bed at Nelsons, a cattleman. Cold.**

Bert **Left at 9 AM with a 20 lb. pack for Peach Springs. Hiked 7 hours up the 23 mile trail to the R.R. A little woman at the pump station gave us supper. We**

Emery and Ellsworth Kolb with Bert Lauzon at Peach Springs

were sure tired and hungry. Met three good men of the Nelsons who gave us beds. Mr. Nelson knew Stanton when he came down the river in '91. We sent some telegrams and talked with the Nelsons until 11 PM.

telegram
from
Emery

Peach Springs Ariz. Jan 5-1912

Mr. Ernest Kolb
Grand Canyon
Camped at Diamond Creek out here for provisions All well Telegraph news here at once Expect to reach Needles fourteenth two more up-sets one bad rapid to line yet Rest all easy Send day message Letter follows

Kolb Bros.
10 am. 6th

January 6
Emery

Very cold night.

Sent films by Exp. get telegram from Earnest and Blanche. Nelson boys decide to go in with us if we wait until following day. Bert help shoe horses. We make pictures with Bill's camera.

Ellsworth

Get provisions from different parties pack our films and ship them. J.L. Nelson Peach Springs, Ariz.

Bert

Bought grub from different citizens. Bill said if we would stay over a day he would go to the river with us. John and I shod the horses while Ed and Emery were taking pictures of the bunch. Mr. Nelson was up in the eve.

letter from
Emery

Jan 6th. 12

My dear wife.

Our flour getting wet we had to walk out here and replenish. Sent you a telegram last night and hope to hear some favorable news from you.

We walked 22 miles and climbed over 5000 ft in it.

Each carried 20 lb. films which we will ship from here. We have one more bad rapid which we have to line. Sorry we had to loose the time coming here. We have had plenty excitment since leaving B.A. One upset with Ed & Earnest before reaching Basses.

Then Christmas eve was the worst we had on the whole trip. Ed upset and was floating down the river. I started right after him and smashed a hole in my boat large enough to crawl through. Bert Lauzon the fellow with us was Johnnie on the spot and swam out in the ice cold water and got in the boat. We were all seperated for a while but finally got together in a little corner.

Christmas we repaired my boat which is as good as new.

We will not have much difficulty from here on except one rapid we have to line.

The extreme low water will likely give us trouble on sand bars below. We have figured on getting out the 14th. A long time I know but then it will be over with. We lost quite a lot of pictures and M.P. Camera got wet a couple of times so we could not operate but on the whole feel very well satisfied.

How is my little Edith? Tell her to be good girl and Dad will come home soon. It has been bitter cold. Rocks covered with ice and would freeze on ones clothes as soon as sprayed on us. We have not suffered much though.

Write me to Needles.

With much love to you & baby.

    Your hubby

                              Emery.

                     Peach Springs. Jan 6th. 12.   letter from
Dear Blanche.-   Emery

I find I have time to write again. I got your good message and would have said to write had I known we would not have got away until morning. The walk in was too much for Ed. He had rather a tight shoe and is a little lame today. There is nothing here but one family out side the R.R. people and no one wants to sell any thing or keep any one over night but finally got fixed out. A couple cowboys are going in to the river with us so we may have a chance to get some thing carried for us. The walk does not bother me at all. Our new man is certainly a dandy. I have not cooked a meal since we started and he is as nervy as they make them. He is a French Canadian. You may rember him as he worked for Bass. On Christmas we painted a sign and took some pictures with it in as we repaired my boat. (Merry Xmas)

It was just one whack and the boat kept on going but in that one it broke all boards clear down the side and 2 ft. long. *Edith* is ok now though as she does not leak a bit. I am the ships carpenter. Having Bert along makes things fine and we are all in better condition than on reaching B.A.

Glad you were not up at the canyon to suffer this cold. 17° below zero at Kingma and it is low compared to B.A. Well I don't know anything more and as the train is coming I'll mail this. so good by dear, be good once more.

> Your loving hubby
> Emery.

January 7

Emery   Have breakfast with Bill. Leave for the canyon in a wagon. Lunch at half way spring. Get to river at dark. Cross Nelsons after dark.

Ellsworth   **The two Nelson boys John & Will hitch up team and haul us half way to river then Will rides and packs the other horse and we make our camp about dark. Cross to the North side. Have an interesting day. Quite warm after being out on top.**

Bert   **We left for the river at 10 AM with a team and got dinner. Left the wagon and hiked to River; got there at 5 PM. Crossed John and Bill over, and had a good supper and pleasant eve.**

January 8

Emery   Do a little fishing. Take a little moving picture with Nelsons in it [*An illegible word marked through*] and bid them farewell. Run 8 very little rapids. Come to a little fall on South side then strike a long rapid with very bad dip in it we run the top and then at the foot of this is a heavy rapid with very large rocks all through. We line and portage this one for a short distance and run the interference waves.

Make 8x10 & M.P. of same. We then have ¾ mi clear water and run another small rapid. ¾ mi more we come to as bad a rapid as we have had below B.A. small stream comes on the S.W. or left side going down. Canyon also directly opposite. We take loads out and line Ed's boat down quickly. It was too dark to get *Edith* over so we camp on the S. side for the night. Very damp camp.

Ellsworth

Do a little fishing. Two small salmon & a bony tail.

Take a moving picture of leaving and running the little rapid at ~~at the end of the~~ below Diamond Creek Rapid. We run four good sized rapids the last one being rather bad with rocks and swift water and has a very rough one at the end. We make a short portage ~~Stone's S~~ over this. About two miles below we come to a second bad one with bad dips & reverse waves ~~and~~ We conclude to line it. Camp in little Canyon on South. Line my boat easily.

The granite walls here are possibly the highest and most impressive we have seen in the granite.

Very clear night. Rather a poor camp.

P.S. I knock a hole in my boat while portaging on first bad rapid. It is on the third plank near stern. My boat leaks worse than ever in the cockpit and I must have opened it up on another rock. We have gone over Stone's big rapid three times and it is still ahead of us.

Bert

Broke camp, did some fishing but got nothing but two bony tails. Got some moveing picture of John and Bill as we were leaving. Run 8 small rapids, got to a big one at noon. We thought it was Stone's famous rapid, lined it, got down to another bad one in 30 minutes and camped for the night. The terrible rapid still ahead of us.

January 9
Emery

After breakfast we carried the balance of the load to the bottom of rapid. Not far but over many big rocks. We line *Edith* down safely and got off at 10.10 am. Did not go far before coming onto a bad rapid. Very large dips. Ed ran both boats. Take 8x10. Canyon to West. Both boats hit rocks but no damage done. 2 & 3 not so bad. Then we struck a long one in 3 sections, bad rocks but we miss them. We then have a long stretch of quiet water. Walls very high, plateau narrow and blue limes close to the granite. Most picturesque of all inner gorge. We ran a mile or 2 and then came to the narrowest place we have struck on the Colo.

The whole currant ran down like a funnell and was the swiftest and highest water below B.A. The rapid was not long but is a rapid we will not forget. A mile or 2 more and we are now camped on the W. side in a canyon. Directly opposite us is another canyon very long. Muddy water likely melting snow.

The rapid below us is a very bad one. we will have to line the bottom of it ~~as it~~ the main body of water runs up on a large rock. Not feeling well the bad rapids work hard on my nerves as well as my muscles. Caught 13 lb. salmon.

Ellsworth **Rather a hard carry with our loads ~~and~~ We line ~~my~~ E.C's boat easily. Load and start at 10 A.M. about 11.30 we come to a bad looking rapid by a little canyon on the South containing two streams one clear and one muddy. Conclude it can be run on the right I try my boat first and make it O.K. then run E.C's as he is feeling badly while he takes a photo, run #2 easily camp on a ~~big flat~~ quiet stretch for noon. E.C. gets a 12 lb salmon. #3 a big V at ~~opposite Canyon side Canyons~~ #5 is not over 35 or 40 ft wide about 15 ft fall and very swift, waves are very high but we ride them without trouble (out of order) [*previous rapid below*]**

Seperation Rapid **#4 is at the two side canyons and is divided into three sections. The middle and lower section were rather rough and we had quite a time dodging the rocks and big dips but make it safely. We thought it possible that Powells men went out here. The scenery has been most wonderful and awe inspiring all day. The granite is higher and steeper than our section and the marble walls are set back but a short distance and very high. There is a little snow on top.**

(Name of long cactus found at Cataract; Ocoteo) Chapparall has a tiny oval leaf and blunt thorns. Hackberry has a dry red berry.

We are camped opposite a long side canyon on right short on left. Three rapids just below us Bad water. Muddy stream in canyon on right.

Bert **Ran one big rapid early this morning. Ed ran both boats. We got a 14 lb. Salmon which looked good to us. 5 rapids today. High granite walls, beautiful views, and a mighty rough river.**

January 10
Emery Running the 1st rapid below us we quickly land on the N. Side of river just at the head of the bad one I mention in my notes of the 9th. We

pull *Edith* over a body of rocks and drop her in a little lagoon where we unload her and pack the load to the bottom of the rapid. Just a stone's throw. Do likewise with the *defiance* and line both boats down the edge of the rapid. In this rapid on S.W. side is a huge boulder. The water runs upon it from underneath, that which is seen as the whole effect is of a fountain, water pouring down on all sides. Rock probably 12 ft. sq.

drawing
in
journal

Defiance leaks badly even though we patch her up.

After lining no. 2 we started into one which looked easy. It was not so bad but neverthe less I could not get out of the way of a large rock. Seeing I was going to hit it I turned the stern for it. She ran directly upon it but the recoil waters stopped the boat and it did not touch, simply stopped as sudden as if she had, then turned quickly and swung down beside the rock filling 6 in water in the cockpit and was clear.

No 4 turned just about the same trick on *Defiance*. No 5 was clear. No 6 very rocky. I set up 8x10 as Ed ran *Edith*. Got hung up on rocks in beginning and had hard time getting off alone. When he took *Defiance* he changed his course a little but got in bad again having very hard work to get her off the rocks. No damage done we pulled on about a mile where the river made a sudden [turn] to the South here we ate lunch and enjoyed the magnificient view up the river seeing nearly the whole mornings run.

After lunch we started out on a very swift river through the most rugged inner gorge scenery of the series.

We ran one more making seven for the day. This last one was on extremely swift water and quite long but no rocks. The river here is very narrow. We turn to the west and come upon three very prominent peaks. the river continues to turn in a bow and we see a lava capped es-carpment of rocks ahead of us. We decide at once it is Stones bad rapid. A beautifull little stream comes in from the west.

Lava
Cliff
Rapid

Spencer
Creek

The west wall is sheer so that it is impossible to get down on that side.

We crossed the river and land in a little corner just at the head of the rapid and crawl over the rocks on the E or N.E. side

We carried camp outfit & beds over half way down the rapid and camp on some sand among the rocks 40 ft above the river.

Ellsworth [*Written up the margin are the words* "We now feel sure Powell's men left here.]

"Over hills and valleys deep." Seven rapids for the day. including one we lined. The first one below the A.M. camp was easy. #2 came just below it and looked bad. We rolled a few rocks out of the way and made a channel to get the boats through to the bar of rocks carried the loads and lined the boats Very easy for a big rapid. Outside of a little bank of rocks the walls went up sheer on either side. No 3 was runable but had a large rock in the center. E.C and Bert were carried up on this then backed off again. I did the same thing in #4 an easy rapid and no harm done #5 easy #6 rough lots of rocks everywhere. I run both boats very near shore and hang upon rocks at head of rapid but push off and get through safely. E.C. makes photo. Noon just below where canyon turns South again. #7 just below noon camp is a long swift rapid and good boating for three miles then we turn west again about a mile below we come to lava covered rock on North a stream about the size of Diamond on South and a long bad rapid below. We carry the necessary camp articles below on right and rustle some wood.

Bert Ran a rapid after leaving camp, the first rapid in a series of three. Landed at the head of the next one, and after lots of work got both boats down. Loaded up and ran the last one. There was a big rock in the center of this one. We were in the current and went right up on the rock. The boat stopped, turned around, ducked around the rock and went thru without tipping over. 97 rapids up to date. We got to Stone's famous rapid about 4 PM. We packed our beds and grub to the lower end up over a high cliff. This is where Stanton was headed off for 3 days. We think this is the Muddy Widdica. This rapid is marked by a bold escarpment of rock capped with lava on the north with a stream coming in from the south. This granite section skins anything in the upper granite for rapids and high walls.

I did not sleep well with the roar of one of the most miserable rapids in the series.

After a good breakfast we started to pack to the end of the rapid our beds etc. which we packed half way down the previous evening. We then set in to make a let down. Dropping the ~~Edith~~ *Defiance* down about 100 ft. we pulled her stern on a log placed between 2 rocks with a tremendious flow of water gushing beneath her.

After raising the entire boat on a large rock it was but a short time until she was slid into the water on the other side. ~~then came a very sw~~ There were 12 boulders running directly accross the river at this place. Then came about 200 ft very swift water which the boat had to be manovered around until the place for the next portage was made. The currant pushed past a large boulder with trimendious velocity, and was only by the use of ropes at both bow and stern the boats were thrown behind the rock on which we stood without difficulty. Then came the hard work. Bert just receiving a bad cut in the heart of his left hand was not in the best of trim for the job but he continued without a word. We placed or wedged a log below so the boat would not be drawn under the rock by the suction of the water when she was dropped on the lower side. The work was extremely hard as the boast weighed close to 700. Ells. strained his back on this lift and we were all delighted to see *Defiance* flung below us. *Edith* was handeled in the same way with the exception of a little incident to cheer us up. Just as *Edith* was about to be dropped into the water below it occured to me we were in all this for pictures so I called a halt. As Ed was in the act of fishing a trypod from the hatch all our work was undone by the boat slipping back in the water. An onlooker would know we had pius training as the work was started again without a word. After this we ran the balance without difficulty. It was after one P.M. when we finished the job so we had lunch before starting on. We ran ~~ran~~ 6 more rapids from then until evening. No. 1 & 4 were quite interesting. Camped at the mouth of a canyon from S.W. Fine camp. Mesquite tree chopped by some one years ago.

Granite carved and cut into every conceivable form. Many places resembling a cluster of flowers.

A hard portage and line. Take the boats out over two places in the

rapid. Hard lifting but we finally land them below the second rock. Run our boats to the bottom of rapid and load. Make a few photos. Noon at same camp ~~and~~ leave at 2.30 P.M.

#1 below has a large rock in center with another above on side. Drop behind upper one. #4 is a rough one very swift. Pass it safely. 2 more small ones make 6 rapids for our two hours run. Camp at a wide canyon coming in from the West. Nights getting warmer. Clear. Put up dark room and prepare to load M.P. & 8x10. Out of sugar.

Bert **Lined the boats and slid them over rocks until we got to the last section, then ran the rest of it. Ran 6 rapids after 2 PM, first and 4th bad ones. Took some scouting to get over the 4th one, lots of bad rocks. The stream is a little larger than Diamond Creek. There were twelve big boulders across the head of this rapid. Impossible to run and get thru without tipping over. High granite walls which are high in one place and low in other places. Stuck my hand with a hunting knife, which made me somewhat hostile. Wet all over in the ice water. We ran a place in the river yesterday, not over 50 ft. wide, but big drop and going some. Made 8 miles and found a fine camp, lots of mesquite.**

January 12

Emery Broke away from a very nice camp at 9 am. Ran 13 rapids 2 of them worth mention. Then we ran a great many we did not count at all.

The walls are still high but not much color. The granite gradually grew less in ~~high~~ height. The river became of a different character as the canyon grew more open. Long curves with the water sweeping into the outside wall or bank. Many side canyons and many springs. ~~most~~

Most of the springs left deposites of lime hanging over the rocks & in places the cliffs for several hundred feet were covered with these lime deposits.

As the opening of one side canyon we discovered a cross along the river. It was tied together by a rope and cut with a knife the enitials E.C. or G and NB 1898. At noon we were pleased to know we had ran out of the granite. Twards evening I heard some rocks on the side and looking up saw standing in deep brush & grass 5 beautifull mountain sheep.

W[e] thought we were nearly out of the Canyon and though the

Camp in the final gorge

walls or high walls seem to have dissapeared we had to camp before reaching Grand Wash. In the sand where we are now camped are the fresh footprints of a man. Let it be hoped we discover some one who can sell us some flour etc. as we will soon go hungry.

Ellsworth   Camped just inside gateway of Canyon. 13 rapids for the day 3 or 4 of them being good sized ones most of them being on sharp turns with the rapid piled up against the wall. Ran one with quite an abrupt fall on right side of Island. We took left side and had a short turn below the Island with very little water. No harm done. E. C. sees 5 Mt. Sheep about 4 P.M. and spends 30 min trying to see them again, but fails.

Camp at 5. See fresh footprints. The granite ran out about noon possibly 15 miles from end of Canyon and the walls dropped down to about 2500 ft high. Close to the end they are about 2000 ft high and quite wide apart. Are composed of lime stones with a neutral red tint but principally brown and dirty looking. We have passed many mineral springs with travatine formations all around them.

The fish would not bite today.

Bert   Got out of camp at 9 AM. Expecting to get out of the Canyon. Ran 13 small-sized rapids, 2 and 4 bad ones. Lots of rocks but got over without any trouble. The granite moved down into the Sandstone about 10 miles from camp, or 18 miles from Stone's Notorious Rapid. Emery saw 5 mountain sheep about 4 PM. We did some scouting to get a shot at them but they left. Went down a mile and camped. Were sure we were only a few miles from the end of the Canyon. Saw a man's tracks in the sand; third time we saw tracks since leaving B.A.

January 13
Emery   An unlucky number but one of the happiest days we have had for some time. We got started at 8.15 am. and was but a short distance until we

Grand
Wash
Cliffs

Pierce's
Ferry

knew we were out of the canyon.

Passed the old Pierce Ferry and saw quite a number of cattle & tracks. Passed through a small canyon. Cliffs all stood on edge. Nooned about 2 mile above Scanlon Ferry. Came onto two prospectors Cocks & Brooks. Cocks wore a $5000 pr. overalls. Took snap of them.

Ran down to the Ferry and found a beautifull little ranch. Paid $2.50

for 1 fine rooster 2 doz. eggs, 11 lb. flour, 5 lb honey. We ran 2 rapids & many riffels. made 30 mile up until 3 pm. All feel fine to know the beginning of a smoother stretch of water is ahead of us.

The ferryman's name was Griggs from Hackbery. It was a great treat just to see his ranch. He grew dates, oranges etc. His chickens were most beautifull and best of all the honey was fine. Grigg's Ferry

A young man by the name of Allen came in to cross the river. He had just returned with his 3 horses which had been stolen and regained in south Arizona. An old man called to us after dark from the other side. We crossed him and helped get hay for his horses from the ranch. He was a prospector and gave us about 5 lb. sugar which we felt in need of.

Ran 2 rapids during the day.

Chas. Cox.
St Thomas, Nev. Ellsworth

We live once more. Made a 30 mile run by 3 P.M. and reached Scanlon's Ferry. Spent $2.50 for a chicken 2 doz eggs, 5 lbs honey and 10 lbs flour. Into a different climate. Date palms, orange trees (frozen) etc. This is the coldest winter known. Met two prospectors who live a short distance above, a Mr. Cox who wore $5000.00 overalls & a Mr. Brooks.

There seems to be considerable travel here. A young fellow named Allen came in from Hackberry 70 miles distant with some stock. Was raised in Tuba. A voice across the River has just hailed us asking about hay. Ran 2 little rapids and lots of swift water. The ranch here looks very homey with its sheep, hogs horses, cattle, dogs & cats all well fed and contented looking.

Left camp, ran two rapids of small size. Got out of the Canyon to Grand Wash at 11 AM. Made 25 miles; got to a camp a mile above Greeg's Ferry. Met two men named Charles Cox and Brooks, owners of mines. Tried to get some grub but they had none. Russell and Monette stopped with them for a week resting up when they came down 4 years ago. Stopped at Greeg's Ferry and camped for night. Bought some honey, a big chicken, flour and eggs. Things looking good. Bert

A young fellow came along on his way to Paringo valley from Flagstaff, going home to Nev. Name was Allan Greeg, has a nice litle place, raising grapes, dates, hay, and everything.

January 14

Emery Got started from Scanlon Ferry at 9 am. Ran 2 rapids during the day, one Hualpai rapids, quite large water.

Passed through one small canyon about 6 miles long not named on our old maps. Then the country opened up and at noon we ran to Virgin River and lunched just above it. An old stone house quite large & flat roofed stands at point where the 2 rivers unite. The Virgin comes in through a wide valley very flat. We camped at the head of Boulder canyon. Volcanic action is evident in all the surrounding rocks.

Virgin
River

Ellsworth **Got some more honey and picked some frozen figs. Took a few little pictures of ranch scenes. Started at 9 A.M. reached Virgin River at 2.30. Lunched. 3.30 to 5.30 to reach the deep entrance to Boulder Canyon. Water very low and we had considerable trouble with sand bars. Mouth of Virgin is about 1 mile wide. Water as big as Havasupai. Red and muddy. Peculiar coloring in Black Mts. Very dark rock with large patches white, yellow vermillion purple etc all mixed rocks all show evidence of heat.**

Placer locations have been taken up from mouth of Grand Canyon to Black Mts. We ran 3 rapids to-day 2 very small and one a little larger of local fame called the Walpi rapid. Our friend who called from across the River last night was one of two prospectors who have been located at Temple bar prospecting. We find a large outfit there. We helped him cross some hay and in return he gave us some sugar.

Bert **Left the ferry just in time to miss Greeg and raise the ferry out of the mud. Ran Wallapai Rapids—they were a cinch. Made old Benillo ferry at mouth of Virgin River in Nev for dinner. Camped for night at head of Boulder Canyon. Beautiful formations here of red, green, and all colors—volcanic.**

January 15

Emery We had gone but a short distance in boulder canyon when a shout came from the left or N. bank. On landing we found Mr. Neal & Campbell who were mining for a San Fran. concern. They were fine citizens and sold us the neaded grub to carry us to Needles. They were about 50 mile from Las Vegas. On reaching the end of the canyon which was not over 10 or 12 mile we saw tracks in the sand and as we passed we called. In a few seconds 2 miners came running through the brush. We were some distance below them but answered their quiries as to where we had come from. They told us something about a raft that had gone down the river; later on we learned the party was taking a raft of ore to Needles.

We had some trouble at an island just above Black canyon on the shoals but were able to get off by climbing out in the water. At the head of Black Canyon we stopped for lunch and had a short talk with another prospector camped there. Black Can. proved to be good water for travel and we camped about ⅔rds the way thru it. On the way we passed a raft and several places saw tracks. The weather got much warmer and the sky somewhat clouded. The canyon is much in appearance like the granite gorge, but not high. Water touches ~~bank to bank in many~~ wall to wall in many places. Camped on S. side.

Black Canyon

Camped about ¾ of the way below head of Black Canyon. Met two miners at work in Boulder Canyon about an hours run from A.M. camp. Stopped about one half hour and purchased a few provisions. Learn it is about 40 or 50 miles from there to Las Vegas and 24 from Vegas Wash to L.V. See two more prospectors who tell us a raft loaded with oar is going down the River ahead of us. Pass Old Fort Calville and take a photo of it. It is a stone building without windows or roof and has a number of stone corralls near by. At noon we turn South. Get stuck on bar near large Island below L.V. Wash. Have to get off and push. Camp below for noon. E. C. goes up and interviews a prospector who is camped near by. See some burros come down to the River. Rock in this section looks like slag dumps. Most of it hard without seams and of a mineral bearing quality. Sky cloudy most of day, beautiful sunrise. Camped at 5.30. Sky clear. Warm. Black Canyon has rather swift current lots of whirls and boils but no rapids.

Ellsworth

Good water to travel in. Came to Boopah Mng. Cos. Camp about 6 miles down Boulder Canyon. Met two men there named Cambell and Niel. Bought a good supply of grub there. Cambell staked me to a sack of tobacco. Ran about 4 miles more and got to Old Coalville at end of Boulder Canyon.

Bert

Nooned at a place where two men were camped at mouth of Black Canyon opposite Fortification Mt. Ran 3 hours and camped in Black Canyon for the night.

January 16

Emery About 9 am we got our start from camp. In another hour we were out of Black Canyon.

On our way down passed an old ladder leaning again the S. wall and about 100 ft up the side. By eleven oc'clock we had a mill in sight which proved to be El Derado; here we discovered a Mr. Krozier & Weiss the Supt. of the mine which was closed. We were much pleased in being able to telephone to Search Light Nevada and have telegrams sent to the folks. We departed at 11.20 and were soon out of their sight. Passed 2 miners on N. side. Very hard wind impeded our progress so that we camped 5 mile above Cottonwood island. Here we were surprised to find several ranches with large stacks of alfalfa. We were informed that Searchlight was but 14 mile from the river.

El
Dorado
Mine

Three men one a Mr. Bly spend the evening with us. We are now 60 mile above Needles. 2 days hurrah.

Ellsworth **Start at 9 A.M. Get out of Black Canyon about 10. A short distance below come to old stamp mill at stamp mill in charge of a Mr. Wise & Mr. Crozier. Stop and have a chat with them and use their telephone to send some telegraphic messages out Via Search Light Nev. 23 miles away. A very home like place and two very plesant acquaintances. Spend an hour but beg off staying over for dinner and push on. A heavy wind has come up; upstream of course and makes hard rowing. I get stuck on bar and have half hours hard work getting off. Noon at 1 P.M. on East side. We pass lots of deserted placer and mineral workings. About 5 come to some prosperous looking ranches on big bottom 4 miles above Cottonwood Island. Stop at second place on West and get permission to camp. Wood a little scarce. After Supper Mr. Bly the owner and two other men come out and we spend a very plesant evening. A mining man relates his experience with an Indian who afterwards runs amuck and kills two white men. He came home to his tent house which had been entered by the Indian who had cut a hole in the rear roof and climbed in taking blankets etc. then coming back** after grub. The miner, all ignorant of the fact unlocked his door and found the Indian all crouched ~~down~~ where he had jumped to catch the door but missed his hair all tousled from climbing in and out, a fierce expression on his face and there they stood. The miner was surprised but cowed the Indian until he got inside and got an ax, then compelled him to get his blankets and put his stuff back then got him something to eat. The Indian has never been captured. Mr. Bly put bill into the county for protecting 2 dupties.

One hrs. run took us out of Black Canyon, which is about 16 miles long. Seven miles more took us to Eldurado Canyon and mine. Met two men there named Wise and Bill Crozier. They had been looking for the expedition for some time. Ed and Emery telephoned some telegrams to Searchlight, 27 miles away. They wanted us to stay for dinner but we kept on going. A fierce wind blowing upstream all afternoon. Camped for the night at riverside ranches, 14 miles from Searchlight and 5 miles above cottonwood island. A young man named Bly was the owner. Made about 35 miles today.

Bert

January 17
Emery

Have a chat with Mrs. Bly & children. then departed with the expectation of reaching Ft Mojave. We did very well in keeping off sand bars by means of one of us acting as a stearsman and the other boat following. The river spread out a mile in places.

Saw many ducks.

Arrived at Ft. Mojave. Saw school leave out. Hear band. Gyser. Otter, no fish. We leave Mojave just at sundown and soon found it was so dark [*An illegible word marked through*] as well as being hasarded by a peculiar dazling light that to try and push on would be foolish. Though we tried landing not more than a quarter mile below the fort it was accomplished only by very strenous efforts and was one of the few times we were nearly compelled to stay in our boats during night. When we did get to shore the willows were so thick it was necessary for us to cut the willows to have room for a fire and place to lay our beds. The sand was very wet and during the night heavy frost covered our beds.

Fort
Mojave

Started at 8.30. Both get stuck on bar oppsite Cottonwood Island. Get out of Pyramid Canyon at 12. A fine current and a perfect day. Noon

Ellsworth

four miles below. The last three nights have been warm and plesant, days comfortable in our shirt sleeves P.M. reached Camp Mojave about 4.30 easy rowing. Sent telegram by telephone to E.V. informed Harvey House of our arrival. Camp just below among the tules. Damp ground. All shave up. The Indian band is playing good music.

The river is mile wide here ~~and~~ shoals and sandbars are numerous.

Seminole Apts.

Flower St.

[The facing page of the journal has a drawing of the Buttes of the Cross.]

Bert Left at 8:15, got to Cottonwood Isle, stuck on a sandbar twice got thru Pyramid and Bull Head Canyon before lunch. Passed Carterville Ferry at 2 PM. Good water to Fort Mohave, got there at 5 PM. Made 40 miles today. Ed went up to buy a hat as he had nothing but a sleeping cap for he lost his other one in River at Xmas rapids. We saw some of the officials at the Fort, also the Indian band which was about thirty strong and was good. We went down below the Fort to camp and got stuck on a sandbar. Just made it to shore and camped in the thick brush before dark. This is the 25th camp.

January 18
Emery

Needles
California

We get an early start for Needles and found a better traveling river than the day previous. The current on the west side of an island just above Needles was fine. Saw Mojave Indians in boats bringing wood to town. We telephoned ~~that~~ from Ft Mojave that we expected to arrive at Needles 12.30 P.M.

On our arrival we were met by Dimit with a letter from Beaman to the effect our boats were to go to the Santa Fe Ticket office. We take a moving picture as the town folks come down to see our arrival.

Mr. Silvers the sect to Mr Tuttle invites us to his home and we enjoy the music of Mrs. Dr. Parker. Mr Rylie has a suit of rooms for us and ~~and~~ entertained us royally.

Ellsworth Break camp early. Stop outside of town and arrange our stuff for shipping. Row into upper end of Needles at noon. Friends meet us and arrange for a landing and M.P. later in P.M.

Busy scene Indians in boat, motor boats, workmen on cement warves etc.

4 P.M. automobiles and crowd appears. We row into sight and land. The picture is made. The run is over.

Left camp at 7 AM for the run to Needles of 18 miles. Got on to some sand- Bert bars but made it off without getting out of the boat. We used up our powder shooting for fish, but only came close to an otter which came close to the surface in a hurry. Made it down near the smelter at 11:45 AM. Arranged the loads and pulled into the landing at 1 PM. A big crowd of autos and people met us there. The boys got moving picture of the crowd and of our landing. Mr. Rilley, manager of the El Garces Hotel, fixed us up with a fine dinner, and our money was counterfiet. They gave us a nice little entertainment in the eve. As I did not carry any extra baggage, I borrowed a suit of clothes from the cashier named Demey. Met Mr. & Mrs. Silvers, Secy. to the Division Supt. Ed and Emery left the next night for Los (Angeles) and I came to Kingman, after a successful trip.

H.R. Lauzon

Written in back of Emery's journal

The Reo Grand crosses G. river in the valley where the trail from Santa Fe to Los Angeles was laid out by William Wolfskill in 1830
    Celebrated as the "Old Spanish Trail. Here, Capt Gunnison crossed in 1853 on westward journey and was killed by Gosi-Utes.
    Reio Grand bridged the river in 1883.

The *Coconino Sun* ran another front page story 26 *January* 1912:

KOLB BROTHERS COMPLETE PERILOUS JOURNEY

A letter from Elmer Kolb, now in Los Angeles, says that he with his brother and Bert Lanzon landed at Needles, California, on the Colorado with their boats, January 18th, having made the trip from Bright Angel trail down the perilous river in safety. The trip to the end of the canyon was made extremely difficult on account of cold weather, though no accidents occurred. The two boats arrived in fair condition after having shot rapids and weathered the swift and dangerous river. The boats will be kept as souvenirs of the hazzardous trip, a trip through which no others except Major Powell, ever made. The Kolb brothers are to be congratulated on the successful culmination of a voyage that will make them famous, aside from the great vulue of the first moving pictures ever taken of the worlds famous Canyon stream.

Emery Kolb

A letter addressed to Emery Kolb from Charles Russell is of interest as a climax to the trip. It is as follows:

June 28. 1913

Mr. Emery Kolb

Grand Canyon, Ariz.

Dear Sir.-

I have heard of your trip through the Grand Canyon taking pictures and moving pictures but I understand you did not make a complete success of it.

Now don't you think there would be a good lot of money in making a successful trip through and take enough stationary views of the canyons to give a comprehensive idea of the entire line of canyons; that is by taking them close enough together so that they would show the entire line of canyons. This would mean taking nearly 4000 views. These views could be colored and shown in regular order through the picture machines and at the proper place the moving picture of the boats shooting the rapids?

My idea would be to start at Green River Utah and finish at Needles, Cal. There are about 600 rapids on that stretch of river and making a low estimate of 50 ft. of film to each rapid. They should yield 30000 ft of moving pictures.

By making this trip in July of 1914 it could be finished by December and the pictures could be ready for the fairs in Frisco & San Diego in 1915.

A complete set of stationary views such as that would be would find a ready sale to many people and to institutions, and concessions for the showing of the pictures at the fairs should bring a handsome return I think. You see it would require at least 4 different shows to show it all. Say one for Labyrinth, Stillwater & Cataract Canyons. One for Marble, and probably 2 at least for the Grand Canyon and it would be a show at which the price of admission would be at least 25 ¢ instead of the usual 5 & 10 ¢ shows.

It would be a record of the Grand Canyon that very likely no one else could ever get.

If you think this is worth doing let me have your opinion about it.

I have made this proposition to several moving picture firms but to them I offered to furnish boats men and provisions for the trip and take it through for $10000.

Now if you think we can make more out of it ourselves let me know.

Or if you don't think it would pay probably you can enter into negotiations with some outfit to furnish them with the films and photos for a certain price. You would probably have a better idea than I would what that price should be as I know very little about the cost of films & taking pictures.

I am willing as stated above to furnish boats men and provisions for the trip for $10000 and take the party through. You can probably calculate what the 3 or 4000 stationary view would be worth and the 30 to 60000 ft of films.

I am satisfied going properly equipped we can make a successful trip. As I understand you were not making any money out of your other pictures, but that is easily explained. You made too many portages and did not run the worst rapids which would have made the best pictures, and you were not properly equipped anyway for that kind of a trip. In our other trip we made only 8 portages and had the river been higher could have ran some of the ones we portaged. Probably going in July when the river is higher we would not need to make more than 3 or 4 portages.

Awaiting your reply I remain

Very truly yours

Charles Russell

Sept. 15, 1913

letter
from
Ellsworth

Mr. Chas. Russell.

Mexico.

Dear Sir:-

Your kind favor was received a great while ago but we neglected answering for several reasons: the principal one being that we were very busy adding new material to our films. We have just returned from an extended trip among the Hopi and Navajo. Before that the writer took a little trip from Needles to the Gulf.

We beg leave to state that we are hardly interested in your Exposition proposition. We thrashed that out long ago and concluded people were looking for 20 minute stuff when there; not an extended show. We may be mistaken but imagine it would be a loosing proposition. We had many such offers as yours in regard to buying films but no firm would take more than 1000 ft., and no two firms will buy the same line of stuff if they know it. As for a continuous line of stuff Mr. Stone has such a collection: 2200 subjects. Few people care to look at so many pictures as only about one in twenty made an interesting or artistic picture. We prefeered to pick our pictures and have about 600 subjects, about 400 of these being real pictures according to competent critics. Composing pictures and getting proper exposures in our still pictures was usually easy, for that has been our work for some time.

We had our troubles with the motion pictures, partly on account of our inexperience, principally on account of the poor light in Dec & Jan. The most experienced operator, however will have trouble on such a trip. You quite likely know something of the difficulties to be met with.

At that, what film we have is meeting with hearty reception before many of the foremost societies and clubs in the East including such as the American Geographic Society of Washington D.C. and the Buffalo Academy of Arts and Sciences.

We take the liberty of dissagreeing with you on one or two subjects. We infer that you think your boat was the right type. Our own observation is that every person who has gone through and lived is certain that his boat was about right. In speaking of your trip we always gave you credit for having unlimited nerve for attempting it in such a boat. We believe you have a record of starting with three boats and loosing them all before you had covered half the rapids, and only recovered the last one by chance.

Three parties have used boats similar to ours—Galloway, Stone, and ourselves. Every boat but one finished at Needles. This one is at Hite; in perfect condition. I saw Galloway's boat at Parker two months ago, looking as good as new. When my brother and I go down again we will use the same boats we used on our first trip.

You also seem to infer that, because we got through we failed to run the rapids. Without farther comment we will give you a little data, which we assure you is the truth.

1. We ran every thing in Cataract Canyon making it in four days running and with out any trouble.
2. We have a motion picture of running Soap Creek Rapid in Marble Canyon but failed to catch the upset which occured. We made one portage in Marble. The 5th big rapid below Soap Creek.
3. We ran one boat over Hance Rapid after portaging the first boat. We ran every thing but seven rapids in Grand Canyon below Hance. These seven were

1. One mile above Tapeats Creek.
2. Lava Falls
3. A narrow rapid about 15 miles below Lava F.
4. A rapid about 5 miles below Diamond Creek- ran the upper ¾s— made a little portage.
5. Two miles below lined a rapid.
6. Lined the middle part of rapid where Powell's men left.
7. Portaged big rapid below lava capped rock on right.

This is our record. Some of the rapids we ran made fairly good pictures. They would be better in a good light. We lost all motion pictures between B.A. Trail & Kanab. We have still pictures of running at least 30 of the biggest rapids. This includes Hance, Monument and Hermit Creek which are not the biggest however. We had four upsets.

1. in Soap Creek.
2. Above Bass in a little rapid of no importance, due to carlessness on my part.
3. 4 miles below Bass. Almost fatal to me. My brother smashed his boat coming to my assistance. Boat was repaired Xmas day and is as good as new.
4. Last upset in a short rapid in a short granite section with two waves.

To refer to the pictures again you might write to Galloway. He has been offering his services with boats for $3000.00 to the Motion Picture Co's. but so far with out a taker; they don't consider it important enough.

We expect to do some of it over again in the summer, so as to get a good light. We will take a cook and a motion picture operator.

We recently succeeded in getting into Rainbow Natural Bridge with our M.P. Camera, and went down to the river at that point. If you should be going down at any time we might help you locate the Bridge.

You will be pleased to learn that our show is succeeding, but it takes more variety than a mere river trip to make it do so.

Thanking you for your interest and with best wishes I am

Very truly yours
Ellsworth L. Kolb.

Dec. 20, 1913

letter
from
Russell

Mr. Ellsworth Kolb.

Grand Canyon Ariz.

Dear Sir.-

If your statements are true as you say they are I was certainly mis-informed about your pictures.

I was told you had made nearly 150 portages and I knew that if that was so you had not run the worst rapids which would have made the best pictures.

I was also told that your moving pictures were no good.

But if your statements are true as you say they are I see no reason for making another trip. So I have decided to abandon my project.

Although I had one fairly good offer from one moving picture concern. But of course if your pictures are doing well I see no reason for trying to secure any more.

The next time I should chance to be in the United States I should be pleased to see your pictures.

With best wishes, I remain

Yours very truly
Charles Russell[19]

c/o Banco Occidental

Mazatlan Sinaloa, Mex.

c/o San Luis Mining Co.

The Kolb moving picture and the hand-tinted lantern slides were carried across the United States in an illustrated lecture tour from 1912 until after World War I. In 1915 an auditorium was added to the little studio on the rim and the lectures were given daily in the studio during the summer tourist season. During the winter months Emery again lectured in the East. In 1925 a second addition was added to the studio and the show was presented there until Emery's death, virtually unchanged. It was updated after the 1921 and 1923 river survey trips and again after the trip to search for the honeymoon couple who disappeared in December 1928.

Emery and Ellsworth dissolved their partnership in 1924. Ellsworth moved to California, where he died in 1960—the same year Blanche passed on. Emery died in 1976 at the age of 95. Both brothers are buried in the Grand Canyon Cemetery. The Kolb Studio, now restored, remains, clinging to the canyon edge at the head of the Bright Angel Trail.

~ *finis* ~

Kolb Studio, circa 1914

The Brave Ones

1 Charles Silver Russell and Edwin R. Monett completed a trip through Cataract and Grand Canyons in 1907.

2 David Dexter Rust founded Rust's Camp, later known as Phantom Ranch. He traveled extensively on the flatwater portions of the Colorado.

3 Nathaniel Galloway is credited with devising the stern-first method of rowing whitewater and using flat-bottomed, upturned boats in rapids. He guided Julius F. Stone down the Green and Colorado in 1909.

4 Linwood, Utah, was submerged by Flaming Gorge Reservoir in the 1960s.

5 Mountains in Yosemite.

6 John Jarvie ran a store in Brown's Park. He was murdered by George Hood in July 1909, and set adrift in his boat.

7 Mrs. Chew. The Chews also owned a ranch at Echo Park. See page 58–59.

8 Pat Lynch was a hermit who lived in the Echo Park (also called Pat's Hole) area from the late 1870s through 1917.

9 Denis Julien was a French-speaking trapper who frequented the Green and Colorado River area in the 1830s.

10 Ellsworth mailed Ms. Koppe a copy of their hand-colored photo album and received a postcard of thanks.

11 Navajo Chief Hoskininni showed his friend Cass Hite (whom he called "Hosteen Pish-la-kai") a river crossing at Trachyte Creek in 1883. Cass called it Dandy Crossing (later Hite) but soon moved downstream to Ticaboo Creek, where he died in 1914. His brother John remained and ran the post office. Albert "Bert" Loper met Hite as he boated through in 1907 with Russell and Monett. Loper lingered in Glen Canyon; Russell and Monett continued through Grand Canyon. Loper returned upriver and settled at Red Canyon, a few miles below Ticaboo.

12 The Kolbs were looking for Music Temple, where Major Powell's crewmen O.G. and Seneca Howland and Bill Dunn inscribed their names in 1869.

13 This boat was named the *Charles H. Spencer* after its owner. Spencer, a miner, hoped to haul coal downriver from Warm Creek, but the boat could not carry enough coal for a return trip. The boat's remains are still visible at low water.

14 Mormon pioneer John D. Lee founded the ferry. He was later executed for his part in the Mountain Meadows Massacre.

15 Frank M. Brown drowned a mile below Soap Creek Rapid in 1889. His railroad survey was completed the following year by Robert Brewster Stanton.

16 Ralph Cameron owned the Bright Angel Trail as a mining claim and charged a toll for its use. He allowed the Kolbs to build their studio on his land. Although he lost his 1911 bid for re-election as a territorial delegate to Congress, he was elected to the U.S. Senate in 1920.

17 William Wallace Bass built the Bass Trail in the late 1880s and operated mining an tourist enterprises there for the next half century. Bert Lauzon married his daughter Edith.

18 John Waltenberg worked as a miner for many years, reportedly for little or no pay. He also worked as a surveyor for Levi Noble's topographic mapping of the Shinumo Creek region. Noble named Walthenberg Rapid after him, mispelling it for posterity.

19 Russell returned to the river to make movies in 1914–15. He lost 4 of 5 boats, and got little usable film. By 1920 he was in an institution for the insane.

photograph credits

ALL PHOTOGRAPHS and journals are part of the Emery C. Kolb Collection at Northern Arizona University Cline Library, and are printed courtesy of Emery Lehnert. Call numbers for the photographs are as follows.

FRONT COVER, IV	NAU.PH.568.3437	93	NAU.PH.568.5750
IX	NAU.PH.568.5787	108	NAU.PH.568.827
X	NAU.PH.568.1130	110	NAU.PH.568.5744
XIX	NAU.PH.568.5821	114	NAU.PH.568.58
9	NAU.PH.568.808	129	NAU.PH.568.3437B
35	NAU.PH.568.9627	131	NAU.PH.568.965
38	NAU.PH.568.1095	136	NAU.PH.568.923
41	NAU.PH.568.4764	138	NAU.PH.568.5791
49	NAU.PH.568.982	140	NAU.PH.568.5806
50	NAU.PH.568.916	143	NAU.PH.568.268
53	NAU.PH.568.1036	153	NAU.PH.568.931
55	NAU.PH.568.3464	162	NAU.PH.568.962
63	NAU.PH.568.984	168	NAU.PH.568.1199
72	NAU.PH.568.3448		

acknowledgments

FIRST AND FOREMOST, thanks to Bill Suran for his tireless work on the Kolb documents, and to Sibyl, his wife, for her help, support, and great cookies. Thanks to Jeri Ledbetter, who has aided and abetted, corrected and critiqued this enterprise, and went the extra thousand miles to index this volume and help cross-check the transcriptions. Thanks also to Northern Arizona University Cline Library's Special Collections staff for their help and support: Karen Underhill, Bradford Cole, Gwen Pattison, and Richard Quartaroli. And finally, thanks to Emery Lehnert, grandson of Emery Kolb, without whose support this could not have gone to press.

Brad Dimock, Fretwater Press

Variants on a Tome:
A Journey *Through the Grand Canyon*

by Richard D. Quartaroli
Special Collections Librarian
Northern Arizona University Cline Library

With the 1976 death of Emery, the last Kolb brother, Ellsworth's *Through the Grand Canyon from Wyoming to Mexico* slipped out of print after twenty-seven unique press runs. At that time some book dealers paid attention to the "Kolb" print dates, even describing each of the two October 1914 editions—one has 48 photograph plates, the other 72—as "first, thus," but few distinguished between them or signatures of the two brothers, Ellsworth L. and Emery C. as authors. The elder Ellsworth wrote the book, with both brothers taking photographic credit. Now that you are holding a transcription of the brothers' journals, you may compare them with the book and find that Ellsworth often used Emery's words in publication.

Haunting used-book stores in the 1980s, I grew curious as to which October 1914 "Kolb" was the true first. I began conferring with collectors and dealers, comparing books in libraries, and obtaining others through interlibrary loan. Although lacking many of the "points" of which my bibliography now

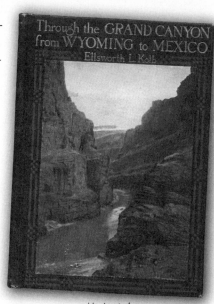

Variant A
October 1914 edition

consists, in 1991 I printed my first list, interestingly enough containing 28 of the 29 known variants, lacking only the corrected 1989. A bibliography course in graduate school at the University of Texas, taught by Dr. Michael Winship, grandson of bibliographer George Parker Winship, allowed me to further refine the list.

Bibliophiles began to request copies of my list in order to double-check their holdings, and several, including this author, became obsessed with the search and acquisition. Dan and Diane Cassidy, owners of Five Quail Books—dealing in new, used, and rare Grand Canyon books—became the first to obtain all 29 known variants. They sold the set to a private collector. There are two other complete sets in private hands, and one set at Northern Arizona University Cline Library Special Collections and Archives.

A few "points" of discussion should begin with the aforementioned "firsts." *The Publishers' Weekly* of November 7, 1914 (p. 1449) stated "with 48 plates," issued in October, $2.00 net, boxed. An October 22, 1914 bill from The Macmillan Company to Ellsworth (Kolb Collection, folder 384) is confirmation itemizing the "cost of manufacturing the Special Edition" of 1880 copies with "24 half-tones special edition," to increase the plate count to 72. Two orders, "for $5.50 for which please send me one copy of the signed edition and one copy of the ordinary edition" and "Will you please send me one of each edition—the $2.00 and the $3.50" (folders 376 and 305), indicate that

Signatures of Ellsworth Kolb, Emery Kolb, and Emery Kolb signing for both brothers

Ellsworth L. Kolb's
Through the Grand Canyon from Wyoming to Mexico
The Macmillan Company, publishers
A LIST OF KNOWN VARIANTS

compiled by Richard D. Quartaroli
with verification assistance

	Title Page Date	Title Page Verso Date	Copyright Date	Printing	Number of Plates[7]	Notes
A	1914	Oct 1914	1914		48	[1] *New Edition on*
B	1914	Oct 1914	1914		72	*spine and Title*
C	1914	Dec 1914	1914	Reprint	48	*Page*
D	1915	Jun 1915	1914	New Ed.[1]	72	[2] *New Edition on*
E	1915	Oct 1915	1914	New Ed.[2]	36	*spine only*
F	1920	Oct 1915	1914		72	[3] *New Edition on*
G	1927	Apr 1927	1914	Reprint[3]	76	*Title Page;*
H	1928	Sep 1928	1914	Reprint[3]	76	*reprinted with*
I	1930	Aug 1930	1914	Reprint[3]	76	*date on verso*
J	1934	Oct 1934	1914	Reprint[3]	76	[4] *New Edition on*
K	1936	May 1936	1914	Reprint[3]	76	*Title Page; Pub-*
L	1937	Feb 1937	1914	Reprint[3]	76	*lished October*
M	1938	Dec 1938	1914	Reprint[3]	76	*1914 with*
N	1940	May 1940	1914	Reprint[3]	76	*Printing and*
O	1941	Sep 1941	1914	Reprint[3]	76	*Date on verso*
P	1944	Mar 1944	1914, 1942	Reprint[3]	76	[5] *Paperback*
Q	1946	Jan 1946	1914, 1942	Reprint[3]	76	*reprint by*
R	1946	Oct 1946	1914, 1942	Reprint[3]	76	*University of*
S	1947	Oct 1947	1914, 1942	Reprint[3]	76	*Arizona Press*
T	1952	1952	1914, 1942	12th[4]	76	[6] *Paperback re-*
U	1958	May 1958	1914, 1942	13th[4]	76	*print by Univer-*
V	1963	1963	1914, 1942	14th[4]	76	*sity of Arizona*
W		1965	1914, 1942	15th[4]	76	*Press, corrected*
X		1967	1914, 1942	16th[4]	76	*version*
Y		1969	1914, 1942	17th[4]	76	
Z		1970	1914, 1942	18th[4]	76	[7] *The number of*
AA		1971	1914, 1942	19th[4]	76	*photographs per*
BB		1989	1989	wraps[5]	[29]	*plate varies from*
CC		1989	1989	wraps[6]	[29]	*one to three*

for $3.50 you received the "special edition," signed, or perhaps with a tucked-in, Ellsworth-signed photograph of both brothers (*author's possession*). The final hardcover price rose to $7.00 in the 1960s.

Textually there appear to be no changes, however after the 1914 variants, "A-C," Owen Wister's "Foreword" is altered. Replacing "twofold courage" with "dogged courage" at the beginning, and removing over 300 words at the end, are the result of a compromise between Emery and the Atchison, Topeka & Santa Fe Railway. Advertisements for other Macmillan books appeared in "A-E," and beginning with "K" a page on the brothers' involvement with the 1920s U.S. Geological Survey river trips is included. From holdings and order records, all hardcover "A-AA" are assumed to have been issued with dust jackets.

World War II rationing and shortage of supplies caused changes in the publication industry. No pictorial color cover occurred in 1944's "P," but reappeared in the next variant after the war, to be removed in "X-AA." "P-T" contained a "War Format" page noting the plates were now at the end of the text rather than inserted within. Plates remained in this location without the note throughout the hardcover of "AA." The number of plates, most containing one photograph but varying up to three, changed in the two "firsts" but returned to 48 in "C," upped to 72 in "D," halved in "E" to 36 for a yet unknown reason, back to 72, then settled on 76 for the remainder of the Macmillan years.

In 1989, the University of Arizona Press reprinted "Kolb" in paperback, using a Cline Library Special Collections loan copy. Not reproducing "all the photographs in the original edition," there is a count of 29 plates, not including the *Frontispiece*. Returning to Wister's original "Foreword," the Press added an "Introduction" by former river runner Barry Goldwater. Since Goldwater knew Emery better, misspelling it Emory, he wrote about him more, leading the editorial staff to incorrectly re-assign authorship in "BB." In "CC," Ellsworth regained prominence.

Since the identification of 29 variants over ten years ago, no additional variants have surfaced. If readers discover others not contained on the accompanying list, also found online in Earle E. Spamer's *Bibliography of the Grand Canyon and Lower Colorado River*, please contact Fretwater Press.

index